"Fathers are more important tha[...] has been fixated on making every service a festival. Consequently, the children of God in the church are unfettered and unfathered. Jack has been one of the spiritual fathers in my life for 20 years. Accordingly, his book is not a cute preaching series, but a life message. I am a more Christlike man due to his direct influence, and am grateful that he is sharing his story. For the fatherless and the father to be, we all need this truth."

DAVID ENGLEHARDT
Pastor, Lawyer, author *Good Kills*

"Pastor Jack writes from a transparent and broken place on the subject of a father's heart. He does an amazing job of weaving his life experience and the Scriptures together to teach us about God's healing power, giving us a new perspective on the Father's heart and what biblical ministry should look like in the post-COVID era of the church."

MICHAEL ESPOSITO
Director of Regional Reclaim Ministries International

"From the first time I met Jack in 1988 I knew I was going to become a champion. I was not a church girl. I was broken. I was wounded. I was less than. I wandered into the church where he was the youth pastor and I instantly knew that for the first time in my life, I mattered. Jack has a way about him that allows others to know they are safe, to know they can be secure, to know they have value. Through the years, Jack has proven that people are the priority of Jesus. He has lived a life evident of this very thing. He has walked through healing without shame, knowing that the goal would be wholeness. He is instrumental in many lives being changed simply because he trusts that God's ways are best. Skip ahead 33 years. My husband, Troy, and I are in our 25th year of full-time ministry. I'm still not a church girl. I'm a whole, healed, and valuable God's girl. Troy and I are currently pastoring in Coeur d'Alene, Idaho where we have raised our three children. My husband and I know that Jack's intentionality in my life is all I needed to do great things for Jesus. This is our goal today with our church. We will love people, we will care for people and we will tell them of their value. We will walk with them through dark times, confusing times and uncertain times and watch God do miracles in their lives. This is exactly what Jack did for me in 1988. Jack pointed me to Jesus to receive my own healing and walked with me through the toughest of times. I believe that as you read this book, it will be the same for you. Just like a seventeen-year-old girl wandering into a church one day many years ago."

PASTOR (TROY AND) DEBBIE CARPENTER
Journey Church, Coeur d'Alene, Idaho

HEAVEN'S HIGHEST
PRIORITY

JACK SHUMATE

Inscribe Press
Creativity Unleashed

Published by Inscribe Press, Hillsboro, OR
Cover by Pelton Media Group, Fredericksburg, VA
Printed in the United States of America

For more information, please visit www.influentialleadership.site
Email the author at jack@influentialleadership.info

ISBN 978-1-951611-45-3 (paperback)

CONTENTS

ACKNOWLEDGEMENTS

THIS BOOK IS a part of my journey towards healing as well as my awareness to live life as a son and not an orphan. Our journey towards healing and wholeness involves many people—too many to mention and thank here. I first want to thank the Father, Son, and Holy Spirit for everything. Words will never be able to describe my love, only a life on fire will illuminate what God has truly done for me. I want to thank my wife and my kids for always loving me, believing the best in me, and living with me without murdering me; especially my wife. I want to thank the incredible leadership team and true friends I serve alongside with at The Loft. I want to thank the incredible family at The Loft that have stood faithful through all my mess, failures, mistakes, healing, victories, pandemic, and church changes. Thank you Loft family for loving me and my family well. Thank you for taking a risk with us as we love people for who they are and as they are, but not leaving them where they are. Lastly to the three men who impacted my life and forever changed how I see myself. Three men who are now with Jesus: Dale Galloway, Don Weber, and Dick Mills. Their influence in my life will live on in how I choose to love people and help others see their true significance and discover their real identity.

INTRODUCTION

The curse of fatherlessness is the result of a false identity.

He will turn the hearts of the fathers to their children, and the
hearts of the children to their fathers [a reconciliation produced
by repentance], so that I will not come and strike the land with a
curse [of complete destruction]." Malachi 4:6, AMP

I HAVE A burden. A burden for fathers; a burden that every man
will know who he really is. I want us to know our identity, our significance, and our purpose.

Our Father cares deeply for each of us. If we do not know who
we are, we don't know why we are on the earth or what we are assigned to do. We even question our identity, worth, and value, causing us to look to our work, ministry, money, talent, position, or title
to give us a false sense of value. We end up comparing ourselves
to the lives and achievements of others. Often we give up, disil-
lusioned and discouraged, willing to live below our potential and
settle for mediocrity.

I believe finding right identity always begins with a healthy
family environment.

Fatherlessness and the breakdown of the family have impacted our nation and world; and tragically, the church, leaving people
hopeless, insecure, and broken. I believe one of the roots perpetu-

ating fatherlessness is that people do not know how good God is or how much He truly loves them. Many people also don't really know who they are, or how God sees them.

Fathers affirm our identity. When people are not fathered, they don't know their true identity as sons and daughters.

The National Center for Fathering

+ 63% of youth suicides are from fatherless homes (U.S. Dept. Of Health/Census) – five times the average.
+ 90% of all homeless and runaway children are from fatherless homes – thirty-two times the average.
+ 85% of all children who show behavior disorders come from fatherless homes – twenty times the average. (Center for Disease Control)
+ 80% of rapists with anger problems come from fatherless homes –fourteen times the average. (Justice & Behavior, Vol. 14, p. 403-26)
+ 71% of all high school dropouts come from fatherless homes – nine times the average. (National Principals Association Report)
+ Father Factor in Education – Fatherless children are twice as likely to drop out of school.
+ 75% of all adolescent patients in chemical abuse centers come from fatherless homes – ten times the average.

When Jesus came to the earth, He came to show us the heart of His Father. He even told us to approach God using the name "Father" when we pray. "Our Father in heaven…" (Matthew 6:9). Jesus came to introduce us to a loving Father—not an angry Father. He came to show us the way back to our Father and rescue us from death, destruction, hopelessness, sin, and fatherlessness. Jesus came to win an orphaned planet back to a love-struck Father. God wants His kids back—all of His kids—and He chooses to partner with His church in communicating His heart and His message by modeling His love. I believe we face a problem in the church by failing to communicate that message and model God's love in the correct way. The new wine skin the church is moving into in this season is reparenting the orphan heart.

When a bride walks down the wedding aisle, she walks arm-in-arm with her father. The father presents her to the groom. There is nothing more powerful and more moving at a wedding than watching a beautiful and glorious bride come down the aisle with her father.

The Lord is coming back for a glorious church! A beautiful, radiant bride without flaw or wrinkle, arm and arm with her Father (Ephesians 5:27).

Today we see families divided and powerless, undergoing a radical shift in composition and definition by the world. This has caused a breakdown in society, and it has impacted our churches. Many people don't even want attend church and they don't see the need to be involved in a church. I believe much of this is because the church has been living as orphans, with a fatherless mindset. Individuals outside the church do not know or understand the goodness of God because many in the church doubt or disbelieve in the goodness of God; so many live with an incorrect view of God, not realizing He is a good Father.

As I write this our world is currently experiencing a pandemic. People are afraid, isolated, and discouraged. Now, more than ever, our families have an opportunity to express the love of Christ and release hope. As I scroll through my social media page I see some in the body of Christ accusing others, demanding their rights, cursing cities and government officials, as well as promoting their political party above advancing the Kingdom of heaven. My heart aches when I read many of the posts from well-meaning Christians on platforms such as Facebook. What if we found ways to serve our neighbors and our cities? What if we shifted our focus away from declaring that the world is going to hell, and started loving the hell out of those caught in grip of the world?

We can. It all begins with us believing in and living from the goodness of God. We can learn to walk in our true identities as His sons and daughters, fulfilling our mission as His family. This book is about my personal journey of discovery: how I became a son and not just His servant. It is about how I believed, not just what I believed. I had to learn to love myself correctly, so I could love my family, and others, effectively.

This journey is teaching me to love my wife, my family, and others through knowing who I am and not finding my identity or purpose in what I do. I write about my journey as a pastor, a believer, a husband, and a father. This book is filled with stories and testimonies from others as well: stories about others who have been loved well and because of the Father's love, have learned to love like the Father. It is about right relationship with God and right relationships with others.

This book is about what's most important to the heavenly Father: us.

So, here is my attempt at telling a story, my story, and the stories of others who have experienced the heart of the Father. My desire is that everyone would experience the Father's love and see Him as He truly is.

The world is watching, creation is waiting, and the best is yet to come (Romans 8:19).

JACK SHUMATE

CHANGE IS NECESSARY

Fear is embracing the inferior instead of the superior.

I BLINKED HOT tears and swallowed hard, holding on to the counter in front of me the day it felt like my world was crashing in on me.

My oldest daughter stood in front of me in our kitchen on a crisp fall day, and I trembled as I heard her soft, but heartfelt complaint.

"I feel like you're my pastor more than my dad."

Her words felt like an arrow to my heart, and they pierced deep within me.

How did this happen? How did my role shift from being her father to being her pastor? The role I cherished was being a dad, first and foremost. What changed in my relationship with my daughter? My heart ached after hearing those words because deep down they were brutal, and they were true.

I soon discovered that what changed was me. At the time she said this I was a pastor living in a mindset of fear, doubt, and frus-

5

tration. I was living like an orphan and not like a son, and the relationships that were the most important to me were being impacted by my wrong beliefs and my behavior. I didn't love myself and I was driven to perform instead of being present and being at peace inside as well as at peace with those around me.

What we believe to be true defines how we behave.

If we believe we are orphans, rejected, abandoned and unloved, we will live our lives as orphans and fear will define the world we live in. If we believe God to be angry, frustrated with the choices we make, we will live in a performance mindset. When we live in this mindset we believe that our acceptance is based on our performance. The more I do for God, the more I will be loved by God. When we create a culture with performance as its core, we will need to continue to perform to feel accepted and loved. This was how I lived most of my life, trying to make God happy by performing or by my doing. Growing up I felt that if I could make others happy or laugh I had value and I was seen, I believed that about God, I had to make Him happy with me. What I did not realize at the time was that God was already happy with me. His mood towards me is always good and it never changes! He's happy to see us when we come to Him in prayer. He gave us everything in order to have and to maintain a right relationship with us (John 3:16).

After hearing my daughter share, I began to ask others in my family, as well as those I worked with, how they experienced me. I soon began to discover and uncover that my relationships were not right, because my relationship with my heavenly Father was not right. I was striving to please Him; working hard to make Him happy. Just as my daughter felt as though my primary role in our relationship was pastor first and father second, my relationship with God was servant first and son second—and my sonship was deeply tied into how well I felt I served Him. Believing this lie about myself also impacted my ability to lead effectively in ministry. At the time I believed I had to be present at everything happening at the church. If I was not providing the leadership at an event, I believed I at least had to be present at most everything going on. The problem was, I couldn't do all those things well and I was falling apart on the inside. People around me were hurt, frustrated, and disappointed with me. When I sensed their disappointment, I worked even harder to win their approval. I believed that if I was disappointing people I must be disappointing God as well. I had an identity problem. I didn't know what the Father was like, so I didn't know who I was. Because I didn't know who I was, I questioned my identity and doubted my significance, and it impacted my influence.

I worked hard to prove my significance but the harder I worked, the more frustrated I became. The people closest to me had become the targets of my anger and frustration.

In 2007, a few years before my daughter approached me in the kitchen, my wife and I decided it was time to leave the large church in Portland, Oregon where we currently worked. as part of the staff. I had served seven years as youth, young adult, and young marrieds pastors. We felt led to leave because we had become dissatisfied with corporate church. At the time we determined we were done with ministry altogether. Church, to me, felt as though it had no purpose; something was missing. Why didn't the church look like the church in the book of Acts? Where was the power, the authenticity and simplicity? Church felt like a business—the business of ministry. It didn't feel real or genuine.

I felt like I needed to leave and get a real job: a job outside the church. I had been serving in ministry for over twenty-three years and it was time for a transition, a change! I did not know then that it was the Lord stirring my heart. Change was not just stirring in me; it was stirring around me as well. Often when God is about to bring a change, He begins stirring things up around us as well as within us.

Change is never easy because it involves taking a risk if it is going to have an impact. We must be willing to take an honest internal look in order to have a lasting and impactful external effect.

When we resigned our position as pastors, we ended up attending a church not far from where we lived. One Sunday morning the pastor preached a message about Jonah and the fish. I had a critical attitude that morning and I was not very receptive. I did not like church and I really didn't want to be there. My attitude was much like Jonah's but even in my bad attitude the Holy Spirit broke through. God the Father gently asked me, "Which one are you? Are you Jonah or are you the fish? Are you going to do what I've asked you to do?"

I was a mess inside, angry, and scared because I knew what God wanted; He was asking me to start a church. He did not want me to leave the ministry. How could He do this to me? He knew how I felt about the church. I was angry at the church. I was angry by what I felt church had become—a business.

That night as everyone was sound asleep in their beds I was awake and lying on the living room floor wrestling with God, giving Him all my reasons, excuses, and fears on why I did not want to start a church; and none of them were working very well.

The Lord said, "I want you to start a church but I want it to be different. I want people to be the vision, my Son to be the center, and a gospel of power to be the message." He told me His desire is for people to have an encounter with Him and experience His goodness. He wants people to know their true identity, find their significance, and walk as influencers for His Kingdom. He wants people in His family, people in the world that don't know they have a Kingdom family. People want to experience power, but they also want to belong to a family—not just a ministry. Seeing God's power without knowing or experiencing His love may change someone's situation—or even their mind—but may not change their heart.

HEALTHY SONS MAKE HEALTHY FATHERS AND HEALTHY FATHERS PRODUCE HEALTHY SONS

"Am I tuff now daddy?" I said as I rubbed my throbbing head.

I had smacked my head on the car door as I was climbing into our family car. It hurt terribly, but I wanted to be tough and not cry.

My mom remarried when I was six years old, and my stepfather was a man with high expectations. He believed it was his mission to make me tough because that was the environment he grew up in. After my parents' divorce, I remember being terrified; as a little boy, I carried a lot of fear. I was afraid of the dark, afraid of being alone, afraid of being hurt. My natural father was an alcoholic and an angry man when he drank. I witnessed a lot of incidents during my formative years that created an environment in which I grew up feeling unsafe, angry, afraid, and unprotected.

My biological dad hurt my mother, and as a little boy there was nothing I could do to protect her, so I felt weak. I knew my dad loved me, but his anger caused me to feel like a failure. I don't ever remember him hurting me; he just wasn't available emotionally or relationally. When I watched him hit my mother I couldn't do anything except yell in terror for him to stop as my mom cried out in fear and pain. The day finally came when she decided to do the right thing and leave her volatile marriage. When she met my stepdad, he pursued her relentlessly until she finally gave in and married him. I think she needed to feel safe and protected as well.

Mom was barely in her twenties when she married the new man who would now be my dad. My mom grew up in the backwoods of Arkansas, in a home that was abusive sexually, emotionally, and physically. All she ever wanted was just to be loved by a man who valued her and wouldn't hurt her. Unfortunately, most of the men that came into her life ended up hurting her more than loving her. As a little boy, I took on the responsibility to protect my mom and my brothers. I found that if I was encouraging my mom and giving her the affirmation, gifts, and attention that her husbands didn't give her, it was a way I could make her happy. I took on a role that I was never meant to take: the emotional caregiver for my family.

My stepfather was also an angry man who had grown up in an abusive, violent home. He was the oldest son and took on the role of father for his unruly brothers and sisters. He used force as a way to control his siblings and maintain order and control. Hearing about his family dynamics reminded me of Peter Pan and the lost boys: no healthy or active parental involvement. "Survival of the fittest" was the rule.

Growing up, I found hard work and humor to be an effective means for acceptance and affirmation from my stepfather. I had a huge need to be loved and accepted by a male. I was very afraid of my stepfather but I desperately wanted his approval and affirmation.

One morning, when I was seven years old, he told me to clean my room and clean it well. I remember cleaning it the best way a seven-year-old knew how to clean. My stepfather came into the room to check my work when I was finished. I could tell he was angry because something was out of order. He tore up my room, yanking all the covers off my bed, dumping out all my dresser drawers, and emptying my closet. The room was now in shambles. He looked at me intently and told me to clean it again, but do a better job this time, and he left me alone in the chaos. Tears flowed down my seven-year-old cheeks as I sat and thought, *I will never get this right!*

On another occasion, I had turned sixteen and my stepfather was going to teach me how to drive a five-speed truck. I was excited but fearful as well. As I sat in the driver's seat with him giving me instructions, I worked the clutch and clumsily ground the gears as I shifted. Every time I would awkwardly struggle with the gearshift and hear that harsh grating sound, he would thump me on the top of my head with his knuckles and tell me to get it right! I was afraid to shift but I knew I had to learn quickly or face another thump on the head. I eventually learned how to drive a five-speed transmission, but I will never buy one. I have too many unpleasant memories of a sore head. In my stepfather's mind he thought he was doing me a favor and raising me to be tough—teaching me to be a man. Really, what he was doing was teaching me to hate men, especially authority figures. I remember being really angry. Angry enough that I would hope deep down inside that something would happen to him or that he would not come home. He hurt me and I was horribly afraid of him. I just wanted my real dad to come and rescue me. Where was he?

My biological dad lived about a thousand miles away. He was an alcoholic and he did not have legal custody and he would not have been the better option for me, but all I wanted was a dad to love and protect me.

There was a hole in my heart that needed to be filled by the love of a father. My need drove me to develop a strong work ethic early, and I found affirmation from male employers because of it. I was never fired from a job because I would work tirelessly to prove my value. I felt that if I ever got fired it would prove I was a failure and prove my stepfather right. Fear became my motivation in life, pleasing people so that I would be liked, loved, and accepted. Performance meant acceptance and it felt good. My unhealthy view that it was vital for me to perform created pain, failure, and more disappointment. I could never do enough to fill the size of the hole in my heart. This motivation to perform later affected my ability to be a healthy father to my own children.

The opinion of others was important to me because it affirmed my value and worth at the time. That's why it hurt so bad when my daughter said she felt like I was more of a pastor than her dad. I thought caregiving was what people around me needed most. When she honestly expressed her feelings, I told myself I was a failure. I needed to work harder, do more; but I was exhausted and frustrated. I felt like I was already working hard but it wasn't hard enough. These feelings were caused by a lie I believed; a lie regarding what my heavenly Father expected from me.

Right identity comes from truly believing and experiencing the heavenly Father as He really is. He is absolute love, displayed in His goodness towards us. He is good all the time (Psalm 100:5). When we enter His presence regardless of what we've done, He's happy to see us. He's a good, good Father—and those are not just the lyrics to a great worship song. I like to picture Him standing next to my bed every night watching over me as I'm sleeping. He's watching me sleep, anticipating the moment I awake so He can shower His love upon me as the day progresses. I believe He's like a pillar of fire by night hovering over our beds, protecting us while we sleep; and a pillar of cloud by day, leading us into new realms of His glory and goodness (Exodus 13:21-22).

As a young man, hurting and broken, I found myself attracted to ministry. I could help people and serve God and feel than better about myself. What a great life. What could be better? Maybe helping others would help me.

On the outside I looked like a duck gliding across the water. Everything above looked calm, but underneath I was paddling like hell. I enrolled in Bible college but ended up leaving without finishing, because after a year and a half I was approached and asked to join the staff of a large and growing church in Portland, Oregon. It was the early eighties and mega-churches were springing up all around the nation.

The pastor of the church I was working in had an amazing ability to cast vision. He believed in people who didn't believe in themselves. He knew how to cast vision and release people into ministry; he was ahead of his time. He had a heart for the broken and the outcast.

This happened to be the fastest-growing church in the nation at that time, with over 500 small groups meeting in homes all over Portland. I was amazed and grateful that God brought me to this church, as well as terrified that I would mess things up. What made my situation even more difficult was that this pastor was becoming a powerful father figure in my life, and I didn't want to disappoint him. My fear of failing and disappointing him became so great that I resigned before I got fired. He had no intention of firing me, but due to my own insecurity and fear coming to the surface, I believed he eventually would. I didn't want to disappoint the man and I didn't want to disappoint God, so the only way to find relief from the fear was to quit.

This pastor recognized my pain and the fatherlessness that impacted my identity. He tried to help me, and he truly loved me.

For the first time in my life I had found a man who believed in me. He saw something in me I couldn't see in me.

Unfortunately, my inability to recognize and receive love kept me from believing the truth about love, even from people who loved me—especially male figures. I knew something was wrong but I didn't fully understand what it was. I loved God, and I loved this pastor and his family, but I felt like I kept disappointing him. So the only thing I could do was quit for good and not go back. I was running from myself and the love my heavenly Father wanted to give me through others. I could give love to other people but I couldn't receive love from them. I had a hard time believing love from others was genuine, or that I was deserving of it. The "giver" in me worked but my "receiver" was broken.

In order to love like the Father you need to believe you're a son or daughter of a father who truly loves and trusts you.

Some powerful healing came to me years later when I was older and had my own children.

I was praying one night, and heard the Lord say, "You're a great servant but not a very good son."

What did this mean? Was God not happy with me? Was I not doing a good enough job? I started to become hurt and angry with God, and fear and ideas of failure began to surface in my heart.

I was angry. "What do you want?" I said. "I'm doing everything you're asking!"

After a few minutes of silence, I heard God say gently to my spirit, "Go into the bedroom and look at your son as he sleeps."

I stepped quietly into the bedroom where my two-year-old lay fast asleep. As I stood looking at him, I heard the Lord ask me, "What does your son love about you being his dad?"

I started listing the things that came to my mind: He loves spending time with me, he loves it when I play with him, he loves it when I encourage him. He loves hanging with his dad. The Lord then said, "I love those things too. I want you to believe you're my son. I want you to live like my son and serve as my son, and not as my servant trying to earn my acceptance." He then said to me, "I have called you to be a father to many, but you'll never learn to live like a loving father until you first learn to be a receiving son." I fell to my knees, wrapped my arms around my tiny little boy, and just wept quietly so I wouldn't wake him. But something was awakened in my heart that night.

From that moment on I began the journey towards my healing. The journey towards finding out how to believe I am a son and to live like a son. There have been many conferences, workshops, sermons, books, counseling, love from others, and times alone on the floor with God to get me to where I'm at today. I am still on a journey—not a journey to find who I am, but a journey to live from who I truly am. I refuse to believe the old lies. I refuse to base my identity on what I do or don't do. I refuse to perform for God. I just want to be with Him. Like Paul wrote to Timothy, "My true son in the faith: Grace, mercy and peace from God" (1 Timothy 1:2). Knowing your true identity will produce grace, mercy, and peace in your life. In order to walk in peace and abide in rest we must choose to live in right identity.

Today when I hug my daughter, or any of my kids, I hug them as their father but I also hug them as a son of my Father. It has taken me a long time to get where I am today but I would never change the journey. We need to focus on our journeys and not just the purpose for them. What we experience on the journey reveals what focusing on the purpose may never explain. Part of our journey towards healing and trust is learning to love from a place of confidence in knowing that we are already loved.

God is a God of the process and the journey is more important to Him than the destination. The process allows us to experience His love and see His hand in every situation if we're looking for it. We tend to look for His hand when we first need to look into His face.

Maturity begins by learning to love ourselves correctly. Loving ourselves correctly includes the ability to discern truth from lies regarding who we are. The enemy will always point to what we've done either in the past or now in order to cause us to believe we are unlovable. The enemy loves to pull up our past mistakes, sins or failures and remind us of why we are unworthy to be loved.

When we believe a lie, we empower the liar. Bill Johnson

Change in us begins with believing the truth about our identity as sons and daughters. Personality is an outer appearance (what others see as truth) and identity is an inner confidence (truth as we know it); and both affect our character. Identity is knowing who I am because I know who God is. My ability to take a risk and make a change must be rooted in believing God's mood towards me is always good, regardless of how I feel. It's an inner confidence and security in knowing that I'm loved, and always will be loved, by God.

Satan uses shame as a powerful tool to keep us from believing the truth about what God thinks of us and to entice us to question His love towards us. Shame keeps things hidden so the enemy has a foothold and he can continue to accuse us. A foothold is a secure place to stand. It allows the enemy the ability to remain undetected so he can continue to harass and accuse us. The result of accusation is a lack of confidence, causing us to shrink from walking out true identity.

> As surely as we died with Christ, we believe we will also live with
> him. Romans 6:8, CEV

I'VE GOT A SECRET

"Do you want to see some more pictures?" Alex asked as he pulled out another stack of magazines.

"Sure," I said.

I was six years old, sitting on the floor of a dimly lit upstairs room that seemed more like an attic than a bedroom, as thirteen-year-old Alex showed me picture after picture of men and women completely naked.

Alex's mom Janet babysat my brother and me during the week while my parents worked. She lived just a few doors down the block from our home, but I hated going there each day. The house was old, built just after the war, and it seemed dark and cold and foreboding to me. It was like something out of a horror movie.

And it was there I had my introduction to the world of pornography.

Looking at picture after picture I felt a cold chill in my heart, knowing something was wrong with what we were doing, but I was curious. I felt strange but pleasurable reactions stirring inside me, I had never felt anything like this before. As time passed, Alex continued my education and exposed me to even more things sexually.

I never told anyone about what I saw or what I experienced. I was afraid and ashamed. Pornography became an issue that I struggled with my whole life. At six years old I experienced something I should never have been confronted with, opening a door for the enemy to walk through and torment me with shame, condemnation, guilt, and trauma. Like all shame and condemnation we can't face, I simply buried it deep inside. I knew in my heart that what I was doing was bad, so the enemy would tell me I was bad. Sexual brokenness is reinforced by shame, and shame gains power when we believe lies instead of the truth of God's word.

A TALE OF TWO FATHERS

> "You are of your father the devil, and the desires of your father you want to do. He was a murderer from the beginning, and does not stand in the truth, because there is no truth in him. When he speaks a lie, he speaks from his own resources, for he is a liar and the father of it." John 8:44

Our heavenly Father *never* lies, and the enemy *always* lies. Fathers speak truth, and truth protects sons and daughters. Lies cause destruction. One way we can detect the lies of the enemy is to examine the destruction that he creates around us and within us. Lies destroy trust and divide relationships, while honesty, transparency, and truth build up and restore relationships.

The enemy uses shame to reinforce condemnation and bring about destruction.

The goal of the enemy is to keep us out of relationship with the Father. The enemy is a relationship destroyer, while Jesus is the relationship builder. Relationships are the highest priority of heaven and the destruction of relationships are the highest priority of the enemy.

The enemy uses shame as the bullet and condemnation as the gun. This is the weapon he chooses to destroy our relationships with God, ourselves, and others. The enemy tells us we are bad, and he uses condemnation to tell us God is mad at us. The next lie the enemy uses against us is, "to make things right, you need to do something good." I lived much of my life believing my acceptance *with* God was based on my performance *for* God. I believed this lie as truth because of what I experienced from my stepfather.

The goal of the enemy is to pervert the truth. Perversion is always, "The wrong version." The enemy seeks to pervert our true identity from the day we are born. Called the accuser in Revelation 12:10, the enemy brings accusation against God, others, and us. The purpose and motivation behind all demonic accusation is destruction of life, while the purpose of conviction from our heavenly Father is healing and restoration of relationship (see Isaiah 61:1-7).

The enemy's real lie is: God is only glad when we are good, and God is mad when we are bad. In order to make God glad, we have to do something good in order to be loved.

This cycle of wrong belief causes us to strive in order to be accepted, or to give up due to the pressure to perform.

God's anger is always aimed at the sin, and His heart wants to heal us from what motivates us to sin. God is after anything that comes between Him, His love for us, and whatever keeps us from loving Him unhindered. He is relationally focused at all times and wants us to healed us so we can receive the full measure of His love and all of His favor! *A correct view of God is crucial to understanding your right identity as a son or daughter.* He is a good Father! As leaders, we need to reinforce God's love when others fail and not focus on their failure How we treat and love others can help them have a new experience with God as a good Father. I could have easily ended up in deep sexual sin, perversion, or even an alternative lifestyle due to the pain and trauma I experienced as a little boy. My mom's prayers, influence from other godly men in my life, and my own hunger for God kept me from spiraling down a deeper well of sexual brokenness. As a little boy walking past my mom's bedroom, I remember and hearing her cry out to God in prayer for me and my younger brothers on many occasions. When you hear your mom weeping and praying for you like that, it leaves a mark on your heart. When we pray and love people like that, especially when they feel like they have failed, it leaves a mark on their heart as well. There is no such thing as failure with God; we just get back up and take the test over until we pass. Jesus will give us all the answers, if we ask, because His love is really that good. We have left a mark upon the heart of Jesus, not just upon His hands and feet.

You will never learn to live like a loving father until you first learn to be a receiving son.

CHANGE IS NEVER EASY

Change is the root of discomfort,
but transformation
is its fruit.

THE SHAME THAT was buried deep in my heart from what I had experienced as a little boy was impacting what I believed to be true as a man. God began to expose and heal the deep wounds in my heart, removing the things that made me feel secure and pruning away the false identity I had believed to be true.

One crisp fall day years ago, I sat across the table in my office hearing the words, "You need to take a sabbatical," from some men I love and respect very much. At that particular time, I was feeling empty, tired, and frustrated. I wanted to quit the ministry altogether. These men are good friends and were leaders on our ministry team at the time. It was hard for me to hear this from them, and it triggered me. My perception was that things were falling apart around me, so I was a failure. In reality, things were going well, but God was about to do some pruning in my life personally. The discomfort I felt was rooted in the change that was about to happen, both inside my heart and outside, as it related to our church structure, for my personal healing. The Lord was about to walk me through a journey of transformation. A true sabbatical means taking a break from ministry responsibility, but not relational connectivity. Sabbatical is a time to rest, heal, reflect, and learn to be still. Even the dirt in Israel was allowed to rest every seven years before planting again.

A sabbatical is a time of spiritual pruning and not just a vacation.

TIME FOR A CHANGE

When I heard these words about taking a sabbatical, everything in the church was just starting up again after summer. I thought, "Right now would be the worst time for me to take a sabbatical." In fact, these men were advising me not even to come to church during this time. As I sat there, I thought, "What if everything falls apart? I am the pastor of this church, and not only the pastor, but I planted it. How can I not attend church?"

I also believed I needed to be at everything that happened in the church, even if I was not directly involved. On many occasions, I would show up at a ministry or an event in order to love on people. I am one hundred percent extravert and I never want to miss a party. What I did not know at the time was that God was preparing to change my leadership function in ministry and how I related to my family. The two things that stood in the way were my fear and the unhealed pain in my heart.

Fortunately, I heeded the counsel these men gave me that day and began my sabbatical.

"Well, this will be fun," I said to myself for it. "There will be plenty to do, time to rest, write, hang with my family, and fix things up around the house."

But things did not get better at first like I thought. I didn't know how to unplug from ministry, from doing ministry, and move into a place of just "being"—a place of rest. I continued to do ministry from my home. I would pray with people over the phone, work on emails, as well as post on social media, responding and praying for church people. My family was not a happy family and I was even more frustrated by being at home, I felt stuck at home. When we are so busy outside the home, we don't see clearly what is happening inside the home.

Fortunately, those closest to me were willing to confront me in love, saying, "We feel that you should not do anything related to church or ministry. Don't even pray for people. In fact, get off social media for at least a month."

I reluctantly submitted, and yet I could feel the anger rising inside me. Submission is yielding to another; it is not control or dominance. Slaves are controlled, but sons and daughters yield. Healing and growth will come as we submit one to another; and sometimes, that is how we surrender to God.

Iron sharpens iron if the angle is right. Paul Young

FAMILY FIRST

I began this book sharing how I was standing in the kitchen with my oldest daughter when she told me that she felt like I was her pastor and not her father. That encounter with my daughter happened during the same time I was to begin my sabbatical. Because I was trying to manage, not lead, the church, my family was suffering. I was frustrated because I didn't know why my family could not understand that ministry was my calling. It felt like they did not love it as much as I did. I discovered later that my family did know ministry was my calling, but they were hurting because ministry was consuming my time and impacting my attitude at home. My fear of hurting and disappointing people caused me to harm my family, giving them what was left over, including what little energy I had when I got home each night. I had become short and edgy at home. My wife later shared with me that I would isolate when I got home. When she told me this, I became even more frustrated with myself, ministry, people, and God. I justified my isolation as resting—I needed to be alone because of the weariness due to all of the ministry responsibilities. Sometimes I would be out four or five nights a week. The fear of disappointing man was tied into my identity. I subconsciously believed I could risk disappointing my family because I knew they loved me. Needing affirmation from others was causing me to harm my family, and it was eroding their trust in me as father, husband, and leader. I appeared to be leading well at church, but I was not leading well at home and it was impacting my family negatively. In reality, I was driven, tired, angry, and frustrated. The crazy thing about control is that it's a lie. We may feel like we have things under control, when in reality, things around us and within us are out of control. Because my kids saw my pain, they did not want to share their own pain with me, thinking it would create even more pressure on my already heavy heart. They were trying to protect me by stuffing their own pain instead of sharing it with me. My family saw me reaching out to everyone else, except them. This created some deep wounding in their hearts. For many pastors and leaders, this is one of the reasons their kids walk away from the church, or worse yet, God. We can redeem and restore relationships and build trust with our family, but it takes time and consistency, and intentionally pursuing them. I am still pursuing and walking through healing with my kids. I want them to know they are my priority and my joy. They are never a burden or interruption, or worse yet, second to the ministry. For me, this will be a lifelong pursuit as my family is my greatest ministry.

CHANGE REQUIRES A PRUNING

There is power in yielding to the pruning seasons of our lives.

Two books that changed my life during my sabbatical are *Sifted* by Wayne Codeiro and *Boundaries* by Henry Cloud and John Townsend. I highly recommend both books. As I began my journey towards change, Wes, an older gentleman I had been meeting with on a regular basis, heard I was going to read *Boundaries*. Wes is like a spiritual father in my life and I have enjoyed my times meeting with him. On this particular day, Wes said to me, "I would love to meet with you and mentor you through the book. I love you, Jack, but as long as I've known you, I've noticed you have blurry boundaries in your life."

I knew he was right and I immediately said yes. I will never forget how excited my wife was the day I came home and told her what Wes and I were going to do. She called Wes and personally thanked him.

"Wow," I thought to myself, "she's more excited than me. Things must be worse than I thought." And they were!

As I began to surrender my heart to the healing process, embrace the pain, and trust the Lord, as well as the men he put in front of me, healing began to take place inside my heart. I started stepping into who I really was.

> Now, if anyone is enfolded into Christ, he has become an entirely new creation. All that is related to the old order has vanished. Behold, everything is fresh and new. 2 Corinthians 5:17, TPT

Don't shortcut the process in your life in order to get to the destination quicker.

The sabbatical was the time set aside that God could begin the process in my life in order to produce the transformation He was after. We need to be still so we can know that He is God (Psalm 46:10-11). *When He becomes our refuge, we experience reformation.* This was going to be a season of decrease before He brought the increase to my life.

LATE NIGHT TALK WITH GOD

One night during my time away from church, I was up late talking to the Lord about some of the big dreams I had hidden deep in my heart, asking why I was not experiencing them. These were dreams I had for the church, my family, and myself. I heard Him gently say to me, "When you learn how to say no, I'll begin to say yes." As soon as I heard Him, I just sat there in my living room, crying as fear gripped my heart,

"To what do I need to say no?"

"I'll show you," said the Lord, "but it's not going to be an easy or comfortable journey for you." Letting go is never easy. We all want more from the Lord, but He will not burden us with more until we learn to release those things to which we are clinging. Sometimes we do not carry wisely what He has already given us (Matthew 11:30). While what we carry may feel spiritual and even look productive, if that is not what the Lord has assigned, we must let go of it. Other times we may carry more than we should out of fear that others cannot or will not carry it the right way. We are afraid that things will not get done or that our dreams will not become reality. When we live in fear, dreams are often the first thing to go because we are in survival mode or simply too busy to stop and dream with

God. Often, people who are afraid of being disappointed by God do not dream. But God loves dreamers! He is wanting to challenge and stretch us to dream big so He can partner with us in seeing it accomplished. Like any father, He loves working alongside His kids.

Dreamers invite God into their reality because they know they cannot accomplish their dreams without Him. God wants to partner with us in order to bring His reality into ours.

"It's kind of fun to do the impossible." –Walt Disney

CHANGE REQUIRES LEARNING HOW TO REST

Rest can be one of our greatest weapons against the tyranny of the enemy.

In Luke 10:38-42, we find Martha busy doing and preparing for Jesus. Jesus, the great teacher, was in her home and things had to get done! Jesus sees her running around the house, doing and being very busy. He tells Martha that she is worried and troubled about many things. Martha was distracted with much serving; she believed things had to be perfect.

Jesus didn't want her perfection; He wanted her presence.

Jesus wanted time with Martha! Her motive was good, but her ministry was misguided. The word worry in this verse means, "to divide." Martha's mind was anxious, her heart was divided, and she could not focus on Jesus. Continual serving and working for God without consistent time alone with Him and rest will make us anxious, weary, frustrated, and even angry. Martha's frustration led to anger, not only directed towards Mary, but to Jesus as well. She accuses Jesus of not caring about her and even barks out orders to Jesus in her frustration. Instead of spending time worshipping the One who was perfect, Martha was too busy trying to make ev-

27

erything perfect for Him. Without spending time with Jesus, we, too, become weary and worrisome by working for Jesus. Sometimes, like Martha, our prayers end up with us telling Jesus what to do, whom to change, or what to fix, because of what we feel we have already done for Him.

> But Martha was distracted with much serving, and she approached Him and said, "Lord, do You not care that my sister has left me to serve alone? Therefore tell her to help me."
> Luke 10:40.

Busyness can lead to barrenness. Martha was busy for Jesus, but Mary was present with Jesus. Mary learned to spend a lot of time at the feet of Jesus. Feet represent bringing good news (Isaiah 52:7). During difficult seasons in our lives, we can find good news at the feet of Jesus. When we become still long enough to be present, we are encouraged to dream once again. God desires to partner with us, so He invites us to dream with Him. Our obedience leads to revelation. As we obey what He asks, He reveals what He wants. Beware of the barrenness of a busy life.

When we guard our peace, we can walk in rest.

Letting the peace of Christ rule in our hearts guards the thoughts we allow into our minds (Colossians 3:15). His greatest desire is our ministry *to* Him over our ministry for Him.

Busyness leads to striving. Striving is usually due to not getting what I want or need quickly enough or in the way I want it. Like Martha, many believe things must be planned, perfect, and practical in order to be productive.

Anything for which we strive will leave us frustrated. The Lord often keeps those things out of our reach. He is not an abusive Father, so He patiently and gently waits until we cease from our striving. If we get what we want through striving, we got it in our own strength. Father does not give gifts because of our own striving. We do not earn gifts through our own efforts in order to feel good about receiving them. Jesus already paid for the gifts which He freely gives. We work from His love, not to be loved or accepted by Him. Mary understood this distinction and was richly rewarded for the time she spent at the Lord's feet. The time we invest in His presence, simply enjoying Him, asking what He desires to pour out will produce more than we could ever ask, deserve, or even imagine (Ephesians 3:20-21).

He gives more, not in order to burden us, but to bless us, and to bless those around us, because our Father loves to share. Our striving after things robs our Father from the delight He receives in giving us good gifts. His gifts are always better than the little for which we are striving.

> Every good gift and every perfect gift is from above, and comes
> down from the Father of lights, with whom there is no variation
> or shadow of turning. James 1:17.

It is not about our inability in reaching our goals, but our inability in grasping what He wants to give us.

There is usually a season of transition before the transformation. Transformation is the fruit of transition and transition takes time!

Learning to walk and work from a place of rest is a weapon against the enemy. Rest is not ceasing from doing; it is ceasing from trying to find your being, your identity, in your doing. This is what Mary experienced sitting at the feet of Jesus. I long to sit at the feet of Jesus. It is there I find His peace so I can walk in His rest.

My rest is a weapon against the oppression of man's obsession to control things. –Josh Garrels

CHANGE WILL TAKE US TO NEW LEVELS OF HEALING

God's focus is on developing the foundation of our character. In that process, pruning is necessary, so that the foundation of our character can support the weight of our heavenly influence.

While reading *Sifted*, I came to a sentence that really spoke to me. It was a story about a youth pastor who shared publicly that he did not want his own children to grow up hating God because of him. I wept as I read that, knowing my journey of transformation had just begun. I needed to apologize to my family so the healing could begin. I needed to own my failures as a father and a husband, asking them to forgive me for putting them second, placing ministry and other people before them. In those days, I was a people pleaser and caregiver because of the fear of letting people down and feeling rejected by them.

My family and I can agree that I am not the same man today as I was then. Both as a leader and a father, I have moved from being a caregiver/manager to a leader and overseer in the church. My decision to embrace pain and accept counsel, correction, feedback, and encouragement has not only produced growth in my own life, but it has impacted the church and my family as well. I am seeing tremendous growth in my kids, wife, and our church family.

Asking others to forgive us is never easy, but it is really freeing. One of the hardest assignments God gave me was that I needed to apologize to my stepfather. Years ago when I was in Bible college, while sitting in a chapel service, the Holy Spirit moved on my heart. God convicted me of the unforgiveness and anger in my heart towards my stepfather, which was why I still had pain trapped inside my heart towards men, especially those in authority. Siting in the chapel service that day, I wept, knowing this word was accurate. I needed to forgive my stepfather in order to be free in my heart. The crazy thing was that the sermon that day in chapel was on tithing. I knew it had to be God speaking to me, because it had nothing to do with the message being preached.

As soon as I went home on Thanksgiving break, I met with my stepfather and asked him to forgive me for the anger I had in my heart towards him. He hugged me and he forgave me, but he never did ask me to forgive him. Him not asking for my forgiveness could have caused the anger in my heart to grow even more, but I wouldn't let it. I had decided to not put any expectations upon my stepfather. In that moment, forgiveness was more for my sake than for my stepfather's. When we ask others for forgiveness, we must do so without demand or expectation of their response. To this day, my stepfather has never asked me to forgive him and he may never ask. I have no expectations of him because I am free. He no longer has a hold on me or power over me by controlling my emotions. Forgiving others is more for our benefit than it is the person we are choosing to forgive. *As soon as I was forgiven for my anger towards him, the pain lifted and my heart was free from him.* Before going to my stepfather and asking forgiveness, I never wanted to be around him. After I did so, however, I was free, no longer bound by the anger I had felt when I saw him at family events. Forgiveness releases us from inner torment from the enemy, our own anger, and the hold the other person still had on us.

Change is never easy, but transformation is experienced through obedience to a revelation.

CULTIVATING RIGHT IDENTITY

Encountering our true identity requires
encountering the Father as He truly is.

Everything we build begins with why we believe and how we believe
not just in what we believe.
We must cultivate a new belief system.

CULTIVATE, ACCORDING TO Webster's dictionary, is to foster the growth of, to improve by labor, care or study. It's to acquire, develop, and form. Everything we cultivate comes from what we believe to be true.

Every family needs a father, and the influence of a father is the foundation every child establishes their identity upon.

Even though the word "identity" starts with the letter I, finding our identity never comes from within us; it's established and reinforced by the Father. It is bestowed by Him. Our identity starts with knowing the heavenly Father as He really is; preferably this knowledge is gained by having an earthly father present in our lives as we are in healthy relationship with both our heavenly and earthly Fathers.

We currently live in a culture that is suffering an identity crisis due to a "father crisis." There are so many broken father relationships or non-existent earthy fathers. As the church, we are called to model what Jesus modeled. We are called to love the way our heavenly Father loves, and in loving like the Father we begin to look like Jesus, and Jesus looks a lot like God the Father.

In order to love like Jesus loves, I have to trust the Father like He does. In order to trust the Father like Jesus does I need to see the Father as He is.

God partners with earthly fathers in order to release our heavenly identity and bring healing to our hearts.

God wants us to experience healing, so He will partner with earthly fathers and mothers in order to help bring about our wholeness. That is why it is crucial that those of us in leadership pursue our own healing.

My heavenly Father has brought many earthly father figures into my life over the years to give me different glimpses of what He is like. Each person showed me a unique facet of His personality—something that I needed in order to help me see different dimensions of God as my real father.

Years ago I had the opportunity to meet and befriend Dick Mills. He was a mighty man of God and he flowed in the prophetic gifting. He had memorized thousands of scripture verses. When he ministered in a church, he would write out a specific verse that God had given him for someone. He would then encourage that person with a prophetic word from the Lord. Every time he was with me he would show me some form of physical affection. I remember one time driving with him as he was visiting our church. He was in the passenger seat of my car, busy talking with someone on the phone as I drove. As he was talking, he reached across the seat and began to lovingly rub my shoulder. I will never forget the healing I received in that moment from his gentle and loving action. At the time I felt uncomfortable with his affection, but I longed for it at the same time. We all long for, and need, healthy physical touch from our fathers. As Dick Mills expressed his affection towards me, I experienced being loved by my Father in heaven, because Dick represented God to me in that moment.

God partners with us in order to tangibly express His love to others. As I drove that day, I was receiving the tangible love of my Father in heaven, and He used Dick Mills to express it. I fought back tears as Dick talked on the phone; all I could do was drive and savor that moment. Today, Dick Mills is in heaven enjoying the presence of his heavenly Father. I wonder if God is letting him understand how much his touch healed and impacted the young man he rode with that particular summer day. If Dick was still living today, I would let him know, now that I'm older, how obedient he was by that simple loving gesture of affection.

There are so many sons and daughters in our world today that need to be touched, hugged, and held by fathers and mothers in a pure and loving way. When we learn to receive pure love with a receptive and healed heart, it allows us to extend love to others without expectation, and it brings healing to their hearts as well. I'll never be the same because of the love Dick Mills showed me that day and the many days that followed when he would visit me. He had thousands of scripture verses memorized, he taught and knew the Word well, but that day the most important thing he did for me was to simply love me. Love looks like something; it looks like someone. I want to love others the way Dick Mills did.

FATHERS AND MOTHERS HELP BUILD TRUST AND SHOULD MAINTAIN LOVE

If church is going to look like a family, trust must be built and love must be maintained. I don't think relationships are going to be healthy if we require people to *earn* trust instead of giving them opportunities to *build* trust. Earning trust requires someone to perform for something. Building trust requires someone to take responsibility for something.

When we struggle with issues of trust we can end up creating "relationships" that function as resources rather than real connections.

Jesus loves us as we are, and for who we are, but His love will never leave us where we are.

Pure love is extremely powerful and life-changing. We build trust by establishing healthy boundaries and having clear expectations. I believe that if we are going to maintain healthy relationships, trust and love are inseparable. In our relationship with God trust is a must. I can't love a God I don't trust, and I can't trust a God I don't love. *Proverbs 3:5 says, "Trust in the Lord with all your heart, and lean not on your own understanding."* Often my love for God is evidenced by how much I'm willing to trust God. My love for others at times can only be sustained by the level of trust I have in God as my Father.

I believe that when God wants to increase our love for others, He will allow situations to arise in our lives that challenge our level of trust in Him. My love can only be maintained at the level in which I trust God. God wants all my heart, all my mind, and all my soul (Matthew 22:37). The real battle will always take place in our mind (thoughts), in our understanding (intellect), and our heart (emotions). *The enemy goes to the mind in order to get to the heart and the Lord goes to the heart in order to challenge and change the mind.* Can I trust God even when my mind can't understand? I am not advocating that we trust people who are dangerous or can cause us harm, but we can forgive and love as Jesus did, by fully trusting God to work in every situation and in every heart, regardless of what we see—or don't see—happening on the outside. What God is doing on the inside may take time to manifest on the outside, due to the layers He needs to expose and heal.

SPIRITUAL MATURITY IS MANIFESTED WHEN FATHERS AND MOTHERS LOVE WELL

Mature love celebrates progress and not performance.

The prodigal son (see Luke 15) came home dirty, broken, and feeling like a complete failure. What impacts me the most about this story is the faithful love the father still had for his wayward son, and he dressed that prodigal in new clothes before he had even bathed.

Remember, the young man had just been wallowing with pigs. How can a loving father do this? *Because his father was more focused on the relationship he had with his son than the dirt that was on his son.* He was celebrating the fact that his son had come home; not on what his son had done before coming home. The father was focused on restoring and maintaining the relationship above everything else. His child had come home; that was his son's first steps towards progress and that called for a celebration! (Luke 15:11-32).

Are we ready to love and embrace whoever the Father brings into our lives or leads into our churches? Are we willing to see their true identities, and not view them in their current state? Are we willing to look past the dirt and focus on the gold in their lives? Are we willing to cover and embrace them in the love of the Father, even when they are covered in pig-pen mess?

Jesus shook up the religious world during His time on earth because He came and showed us what the Father really looked like—what the Father really wanted—and He showed us how much the Father loves us. Jesus modeled mature love; a love that is selfless. God wants His kids back, regardless of what they are covered in, or what becomes uncovered when they return home.

In Genesis 3:21 we read that God covered Adam and Eve's nakedness. God went looking for them and found them hiding in shame, afraid and unworthy of His love, yet God covered them, rescued them, and blessed them. Adam and Eve had done nothing to merit God's love yet He loved them anyway. Mature love risks being misunderstood, ridiculed, rejected, and abandoned. Mature love is patient and kind, it does not boast, it is not proud, it does not dishonor others even at the risk of being dishonored. Mature love is not self-seeking, it is not easily angered, it keeps no record of wrongs. Mature love does not delight in evil but speaks the truth to those being seduced by evil. Mature love always protects, always trusts, always hopes, always perseveres; and it never fails. Mature love never takes a day off.

Mature love pursues others while immature love pursues self interests.

"What man of you, having a hundred sheep, if he loses one of them, does not leave the ninety-nine in the wilderness, and go after the one which is lost until he finds it?" Luke 15:4, NKJV

The prodigal son knew his father was a good man. He reminded himself how well his father had treated his servants (Luke 15:17-19). *He risked going home solely on the basis that he knew his father was good.* We must communicate and model the goodness of our Father to our families, and through that model what church is for. When we truly live as real families, we strengthen trust and maintain love in our relationships outside the home.

The world is desperately looking for families that live in transparency, vulnerability, and mature love. Sons and daughters are hungry for fathers and mothers who model the heart of our heavenly Father just like Jesus did when He walked the earth. The world is looking for people who believe that God is good and that He loves us even if we don't behave.

What kind of Father waits with longing, watching for His kids to come home? What kind of God values family and desires right relationships? I may not have experienced this kind of love from my earthly fathers, but I have found and experienced it with my heavenly Father, as well as the spiritual fathers He's placed in my life along the way. As leaders, we can be spiritual fathers and mothers to the lost and wayward sons and daughters desperately looking to be loved.

The prodigal son went home to his father thinking he would work like a servant because of his bad behavior. He was ready to perform in order to be accepted. But when he arrived home, he was greeted by the arms of his father; he was welcomed home as a son. He learned that day that it was his father's love that determined his identity and not his own behavior, performance, actions, or failures. When we learn how to recognize and receive the love of the Father it affects how we give the love of the Father.

I don't have to perform in order to be loved. I don't even have to obey in order to be loved. I obey because I am already loved. I serve from love and not for love.

Why didn't the prodigal father have his son get cleaned up before he dressed him? I believe it's because the first thing his son needed was to have his identity, significance, and influence identified, restored, and declared by his father. Shame always reinforces a wrong identity. Shame will always focus on the dirt; fathers and mothers will focus on the son or daughter that's hidden beneath the dirt. Shame will cause us to perform in order to be accepted. Remove shame and condemnation with mature love and the enemy loses a foothold in your children's lives (John 8:31-32).

> Just as [in His love] He chose us in Christ [actually selected us for Himself as His own] before the foundation of the world, so that we would be holy [that is, consecrated, set apart for Him, purpose-driven] and blameless in His sight. In love...
> Ephesians 1:4, AMP

We were created and chosen by the Father to be the receivers of His love, and to give love and praise back to Him in return. He was in love with us before we were conceived.

Everything God created, He created for us! I was hiking part of the Pacific Crest trail one summer and God spoke something to me that reinforced His love for me. I was on a seven-day hike when high up on Mount Hood in Oregon, I heard God tell me that the beauty I was experiencing He created just for me. I thought how silly I was to think that this was all created just for me. The Holy Spirit then began to speak to my spirit, telling me He put the glaciers on the mountain because He knew I would need the water to drink as I was hiking. He created beautiful meadows for me to enjoy because He takes pleasure in what pleases me. He created the huckleberries along the path so as I walked, I could stop, pick some, and enjoy their sweetness. He knew one day I would be on the side of that mountain hiking, and He wanted me to know how much He loves me, and how well He knows me and knows what I need. I remember feeling so much love and joy in my heart for God as I gazed into all the beauty around me.

How could God know us before we were created? He knew because we were His idea. He partnered with our parents in order to give us life. His love for us is a gift that can never be earned.

WE ALL HAVE A FOREVER HOME

It was the last day of school and all the children were running to catch the bus home. The sun was shining bright in the sky as Tyler hugged my wife goodbye. (My wife is a substitute teacher in our local elementary school.) Tyler had been in her first-grade class during the school year and they had built a special bond. Tyler was in foster care and spent many of his school days in trouble. He has ADHD, so he has a difficult time sitting still and getting along with the other kids in his class.

"Goodbye Mrs. Shumate," Tyler said, hugging Shelly tightly.

"Goodbye Tyler," my wife answered.

"See you next year," Tyler shouted as he raced to catch his bus. One of the teachers standing next to my wife softly said, "It's so sad that Tyler won't be with us next year." The teacher than told her that the lady Tyler was staying with could no longer keep him. She was an older single woman who had raised Tyler most of his life, but as he grew older it became more difficult for her to care for him and his growing needs. Without even thinking, my wife replied, "I'll take him in a heartbeat. I just need to talk to my husband and my family."

God had already been dealing with my heart about adopting someday. We have five biological kids, but we always wanted six. We had lost our sixth child far into a pregnancy that did not go well. My wife believed God had told her we would have six kids, and losing one was a deeply painful experience to walk through. We had so many unanswered questions. Why would God clearly tell us six kids only to have us lose our last child? Due to the nature of my wife's miscarriage, as well as our age at the time, having another child was no longer an option for us. We were blessed with six amazing kids—five on earth and one in heaven. But we always felt a hole in our hearts. Someone was missing.

We thought the story would end there, until my wife met Tyler and came home that day with some surprising news.

"Honey I need you to come into the bedroom. I have something I need to share with you."

I had just come home that evening, and my first thought was, "I must be in trouble." I began to think through my day, trying to recall my words or anything I may have forgotten to say.

The bedroom was our serious place to talk, away from the children. As we sat on the bed, she began to share Tyler's story. My heart was moved and I sensed the Holy Spirit was all over this decision. We met that night as a family and after prayer decided to bring Tyler into our home.

He arrived July, 2011. He brought his suitcase, some toys, and a little black bag he held close to his side. We took him into his new room and began to help him unpack. I looked at the little bag he was clutching so tightly and I asked him what was in it.

"These are some things that are really special to me that I want to take with me when I go to my next home."

I sat on the floor, moved by what he just said. At only six years old, he had already experienced so much transition in his life that he had prepared his mind for rejection in order to protect his heart. I said, "Tyler, you won't be leaving. This will be your home, your room, your house. We plan on adopting you if you're okay with that."

He looked at me and said, "You mean this is my forever home?"

I choked back tears and said, "Yes, if you want to stay."

He looked around his new room, taking in all that his six-year-old mind could understand, and said, "Yes, I want to live here."

We adopted Tyler December 6, 2012. That date happens to be his natural birthday and the judge told us she had never seen that happen before. He turned eight years old the day he officially became a Shumate. Eight in the Bible is the number of new beginnings. I don't believe it was an accident or coincidence that Tyler's name changed on his natural birthday. It was a new beginning for him, and for us. The judge brought the gavel down with a powerful bang on her desk and said, "Today Tyler becomes a Shumate as if he was born a Shumate. He is no longer a ward of the state."

This is just like our story. Jesus pounded the gavel in the courts of Heaven when we chose to accept Him into our heart. We came home to a Father who had already chosen us before we chose Him. Jesus declared loudly in the courts of Heaven for all to hear, "You are no longer an orphan, but you are a son, a daughter, and you have a forever home as well as an inheritance and the run of the Kingdom!"

I must honestly say that over the last few years we have had Tyler in our home, it has not been easy. You can love and adopt an orphan and legally make him your son and invite him into your home, but the real work is in delivering him from the orphan mindset. It takes a lot of mature love, patience, forgiveness, learning, time, and relationship to shift mindsets and help people discover their true identity. It took Tyler over a year to call Shelly "mom" and me "dad."

Tyler came into our home around the same time that I took my sabbatical. What I didn't understand at that time was that I too was clutching a little black bag buried deep in my heart—a bag I had carried around for years just in case I needed to move on. Father was setting me up. He was going to help me unpack the bag in my heart and settle into my forever home. He wanted me to understand my identity in Him, my significance defined by His Son, and the influence I have as a father both spiritually and naturally.

Change always begins with us. Fear keeps us from embracing change because, like Tyler, we must receive healing and forgiveness as we learn to trust and truly love people. I'm living as a son while being delivered from orphan thinking. I'm learning how to maintain love and build trust. I'm learning how to discard old mindsets and get free. I'm learning how to experience new things and take new risks, understanding and accepting the fact that I was chosen because I am loved, not just because I was needed to fulfill a mission or accomplish a task. We were created to be loved. Created by a loving Father as His sons and daughters. Created so He could lavishly and wastefully pour out His love on us.

AN ORPHAN MINDSET WILL ALWAYS QUESTION RIGHT IDENTITY

See what great love the Father has lavished on us, that we should be called children of God! And that is what we are! The reason the world does not know us is that it did not know him.

1 John 3:1, NIV

Merriam-Webster describes an orphan as "a child deprived by death of one or usually both parents." This is one of the reasons Jesus rose from the dead (John 14:18). He did not leave us as orphans. An orphan mindset is empowered by an incorrect view of God the Father as well as an incorrect view of His love for us. Orphans live in survival mode, because orphan thinking is believing you will receive less than God's best. The enemy loves to enslave the orphan heart (Romans 8:15). The Father wants to set us free by adopting us and placing us into His family! We didn't do anything to earn our adoption. *He chose us, and when we accept the invitation He is extending, we share in the inheritance He has provided.* When we come into His family our lives begin to change and we begin to resemble our Father.

Change always begins with my "yes" and never ends until I'm finally at home with Him in eternity, living in my forever home. Heaven is our forever home, and we live from the culture of that home now. Even though we are not yet living in heaven, we are seated in heavenly places with Him. We can live from the culture of the Kingdom of heaven and release it here on earth.

Love is the environment of heaven. When you're truly in love and you know you're truly loved, you respond from love, and not for love. *When the holes in our heart are made whole by the love of the Father, the heart no longer leaks out what God is trying to put into it.* When the heart is healed, it no longer leaks; it overflows.

LOVE REMAINS THE GOAL REGARDLESS OF THE OUTCOME.

The motivation of the heart should be to maintain love and not just obey the rules.

Remember when dealing with your children that there is a big difference between pity, empathy, and sympathy. Pity is an emotional focus. Pity will primarily focus on pain or offense. **Pity can become a pit.** Our job is to lead our children out of self-pity through empathy. **Empathy is a pathway**—a pathway to the heart and a pathway out of the pain. Empathy desires to understand and be aware of pain, but it does not embrace or take on someone else's pain. **Sympathy is being present** with someone. Sympathy is feeling sorry for someone's pain; sharing in their loss without creating more pain.

We have to choose between a pit, a path, or presence. We need to ask Holy Spirit what is needed in each encounter with people; especially with someone wrapped up in shame or self condemnation. Sometimes when we are hurting, or we are in difficult times, we want pity from God when really what we need is empathy and sympathy from Him.

LOVE WILL RULE WHEN THE RULE IS LOVE

Our focus must always be on the law of love, not love of the law.

For example: I know that having an affair on my wife is wrong, but the biblical rule is not my main motivation for not having an affair. My main motivation is that I'm in love with her and she's in love with me. We maintain our love relationship and build trust with one other. Rules are reinforced by our love. My wife and I focus on stoking the fire of our love. I don't obey just because it's the rule; I choose to obey because I'm in love! If we are truly in love with God, we stoke our love relationship with Him and we will obey Him because we are in love with Him, not just because the Bible commands it. God has empathy and sympathy for us, but I don't think He pities us. He partners with us in order to mature us and develop our ability to love the way He does.

Fear is the result of not knowing who He is and sin is the result of not knowing who I am. Identity is cultivated by recognizing my identity as a son or daughter first and not in my serving or ministering. Identity is never found in my performance, title or position. Identify is found in God's incredible love for me without performance or works. It's found in my surrender and obedience as I spend time in His presence. My pleasure is found in His presence and His pleasure is found when I am present with Him

4

CULTIVATING LOVE

For you did not receive the spirit of bondage again to fear, but you received the Spirit of adoption by whom we cry out, "Abba, Father." The Spirit Himself bears witness with our spirit that we are children of God. Romans 8:15-16, NKJV

WE ARE THE children of God, not we *will* be the children of God. My kids do not always behave or always do what I want them to do, but they never stop being my kids, nor do they lose the love I have for them. My love for them is not based on their behavior. My love is based on the fact that they are my kids. Authentic love will focus on dismantling the fear in people. People can get set free from the bondage of shame that holds them when they know they are authentically loved, regardless of how they have behaved. Wrong behavior does have consequences, but rejection should never be one of them.

Fear is a spirit that leads us into bondage. Most, if not all, bondage is rooted and kept alive by shame. The goal of shame is to keep us from believing God really wants us in His presence. The lie is that we have to keep the bad things we have done hidden, for fear of rejection, abandonment, and failure. The cycle of condemnation causes people more pain, so they need to medicate in order to feel better, which then leads them into addictions that continue to reinforce the lie that they are bad.

When Adam and Eve sinned in the garden, the first thing the Father did was expose the lie of condemnation, cover the shame, and restore the relationship.

> And they heard the sound of the LORD God walking in the garden in the cool of the day, and Adam and his wife hid themselves from the presence of the Lord God among the trees of the garden.
> Then the LORD God called to Adam and said to him, "Where are you?"
> So he said, "I heard Your voice in the garden, and I was afraid because I was naked; and I hid myself."
> And He said, "Who told you that you were naked? Have you eaten from the tree of which I commanded you that you should not eat?" Genesis 3:8-11, NKJV

In other words, from where did the lie come? It originated with the enemy, as all lies do (John 8:44). We convince ourselves that the voice of self-condemnation we hear in our head is our own voice. If we truly are a new creation in Christ, a voice of condemnation is not our own because our old man is dead, and dead men don not talk. The voice we are hearing is the voice of the enemy (2 Corinthians 5:17).

TRUTH IS EMPOWERED IN THE WAY WE LOVE

> For while we were still weak, at the right time Christ died for the ungodly. For one will scarcely die for a righteous person— though perhaps for a good person one would dare even to

die— but God shows his love for us in that while we were still sinners, Christ died for us. Romans 5:6-8, ESV

That is what the prodigal's father did. He embraced and clothed his lost son even before he was clean—not even to the door of the house yet; he was still in the front yard! His father was looking for him, anticipating this day. Anticipating the day he would come home. I am sure the prodigal son came home with his head down, declaring, "I'm not worthy to be your son."

Worth reinforces my identity and significance defines my value.

Our worth is always defined first by our heavenly Father and should be reinforced by our natural father. If my worth was not reinforced by my natural father, then it would need to be reinforced by healthy and loving spiritual fathers. In the natural world, our identity is always established by the father and verified through blood. It's the same in the spiritual world. Fathers are the ones that say, "Good job son, great shot!" or "You're a beautiful princess," to our daughters, "I love it when you sing and dance." Fathers reinforce worth through affirmation, physical touch, presence, protection, provision, picturing a special future for the child, and an active commitment to fulfill the blessing. For more on giving and receiving the father's blessing, read the book, *The Blessing* by Gary Smalley and John Trent.

Our value is evidenced in what it cost the Father to redeem us and restore our relationship. He gave His only son in order to get us back; it was a costly investment. *It is not that I am worthy and therefore the Father loved me. Rather, it is when the Father placed His love upon me, it established my worth.* The heavenly Father defined our value (John 3:16). The Father loved us *before* Jesus died for us. Jesus died in order to bring us into a love relationship with

49

our heavenly Father. That love was established before we were born, and when we are born again, we accept that love, a love He so wanted us to experience and know, not just believe.

When I found out that my wife was pregnant, I will never forget all the excitement and love I felt for my unborn child. With every one of her pregnancies, I felt the same for each child. My kids did nothing for me when they were born. They couldn't do anything. In fact, many times my wife or I were up late, changing diapers, and trying to quiet a fussy child. We were doing for them before they ever did anything for us. Even though I was getting no benefit from any of my children when they were my babies, I loved them intensely. *If I, being a human father in my imperfection, have this kind of love for my own children, how much more love our heavenly Father, who is perfect, has for us* (Matthew 7:11).

The Father has placed His love upon everyone and all creation (Ephesians 4:5-6). And His son has defined our value by giving His life. His life determines our value to God. The desire of the Father is the restoration of relationship. The problem is that many people do not know this. Many people believe God is mad at them. Shame, condemnation, fear, and guilt keep many people from accepting His love and accepting Jesus. The message of the enemy is you are bad and you deserve punishment. Sadly, many in the church still preach this message. While it is true that because of our sin and rebellion, we deserve death. But it is not the heart of the Father and it never was. He is a God of eternal life, love, and favor. We need to preach and model the heart of the Father and not the lie of the enemy. I heard a quote years ago that I have never forgotten: *"If the love of the Father displayed by Jesus dying on the cross does not persuade men to salvation, neither will threats of hell nor the promises of heaven."*

There is no fear in love [dread does not exist]. But perfect (complete, full-grown) love drives out fear, because fear involves [the expectation of divine] punishment, so the one who is afraid [of God's judgment] is not perfected in love [has not grown into a sufficient understanding of God's love]. 1 John 4:18, AMP

The more we believe and accept God's love for us and His love for others, fear and control begin to lose their influence. This kind of love creates a safe environment where our families can heal and change. It begins when we model how to love God more. Our job is not to fix others; it is to love them as Father heals them in their mess and out of their mess. Loving well requires a lot of patience. In loving our families well, we let the Father do His work in their hearts.

We can help our children identify where God is at work and what He is after. The best way to do this is by asking them questions, more than giving them directions, while reaffirming their identity.

When our children understand and walk in their true identities, it brings healing to their hearts and influences their lives in ways that will echo into eternity.

In Mark 5:25-34, we find a woman who risked everything, her reputation as well as the possibility of being ridiculed, condemned, or even killed. She had to get to Jesus, whatever it cost her. She stepped out of her house, a place she rarely left. The sunlight touched her face, bathing her in the warmth. The fresh air and the noise of the crowd began to awaken her senses, her heart began to beat a little faster with each step she took towards Jesus; she had to get to Jesus even with the risks she knew she faced.

For twelve years she had suffered with a bleeding condition. She had spent all of her money and she had seen many doctors, but things had only grown worse and no one could help her. According to Jewish law, she was considered unclean (Leviticus 15:25-27). The law stated that everything she touched would be made unclean as well. Can you imagine how desperate her situation was? Anything in her house she touched would be unclean. If she was married and had children, she couldn't touch them. She couldn't go outside, couldn't worship in the temple, couldn't interact with other people the same way everyone else could. She was a prisoner in her own home, isolated. Even worse, she was prisoner to her own shame.

But that day would be different, Jesus was close by, and she had to get to Him. As she walked the streets, hiding her face from people in her community that would recognize her, she desperately made her way to Jesus. She knew the law, she knew that if she touched Jesus, she would make Him unclean as well. She said to herself, "If I could just touch His clothes, I will be healed" (Mark 5:27-28).

As she made her way through the crowd, she reached out with one desperate grasp to touch the hem of Jesus's garment. Instantly she was healed, no more pain, no more bleeding, no more isolation. Immediately Jesus stopped and said, "Who touched my clothes?" (Mark 5:30). I am sure she thought, "Now I'm in trouble." She knew the risk; she knew the possible consequences that awaited her. But she was healed! The pain was gone, her body was whole! All eyes were now upon her. Then Jesus said something so amazing; something that He did not say to any other woman in recorded Scripture: "Daughter, your faith has healed you. Go in peace and be freed from your suffering" (Mark 5:34). He called her a daughter. She was a daughter and not an unclean woman. Jesus did not condemn her publicly, He restored her identity in front of everyone!

Jesus declared this to a crowd that could have accused her of breaking the law. The crowd watched in amazement as Jesus declared her clean and called her a daughter. This woman touched the heart of her Father in heaven, and the Father responded as she touched His Son! The Father partnered with Jesus to completely heal and restore one of His kids.

What an amazing Father we have! Jesus could have just kept going on His way and the woman would still have been healed, but Jesus chose to stop, and in front of everyone, reaffirm her identity and restore her reputation. She was, and always will be, a daughter. No one could harm her now. She could touch those she loved without condemnation or reproof, and people could touch her in return. She could touch things in her home, she could go worship at the temple, go to the market, be with friends in public. In a matter of seconds, her whole life was changed. Not only was her body healed, but her heart was healed as well. She was a daughter!

Our obedience to express the love of Jesus to our families honors the Father and creates a home life that reflects God's mercy to a world that will be forever changed when they experience His touch. Our homes become a shining example of the love of God.

CULTIVATING VALUE

"There is something about believing God that will cause Him to pass over a million people to get to you." Smith Wigglesworth

Learning to love yourself accurately is key in your ability to love others effectively.

"I NEVER HAD a voice, my voice was never heard, my voice never mattered!" This was what Gloria was yelling as I held her hands from across the table. Gloria was in her seventies. She never was allowed to share her voice when she was young. As a child growing up in a large family, she was too busy helping to raise her siblings, and never had the opportunity to enjoy her own childhood. Gloria's father was an evangelist and he traveled around the country, leaving her and her siblings alone with their mother and not much money for most of Gloria's childhood. Eventually the strain and weight of responsibility caused her mother to have a nervous breakdown. Her mother became mentally ill and she was institutionalized, leaving Gloria alone to take on the responsibility of caring for her younger siblings while her father was away.

Gloria and her husband were now in my office in a confrontational meeting with another woman in our church. As we were talking together, I felt I was losing heart connection with Gloria. It was as if she had fallen overboard and was drifting out to sea without a life preserver as old memories and pain began to surface. She needed a father to validate her. I silently prayed under my breath, asking God what to do next, and I heard the Lord instruct me to take both of her hands and pull her back into the moment by telling her how much I loved and valued her, and how important she was to her heavenly Father. As I did what I heard the Father say, the pain deep inside of her from so long ago began to leak out. We had the opportunity to pray with Gloria, and healing came to her heart as the pain was released that day. Gloria and her husband were leaders in our church and they have had a huge impact on my life personally. Gloria has relentlessly pursued healing most of her life. I love that, as a senior, she is still growing, learning and becoming. She knows who she is and she knows how much he heavenly Father loves her. She has a voice now, and because we have a transparent feedback culture in our church, she has helped many others find their voice, identity, and healing as well. She will always be a daughter first and foremost. Her identity is in her value and not in her performance.

One of the greatest gifts we can give to our children is the gift of helping them find their identities, and learn that they truly have an inheritance; from their natural families, yes; but especially in the family of God!

SONS AND DAUGHTERS HAVE AN INHERITANCE.

When a family member dies, they may leave you an inheritance. When Jesus died, He left us an inheritance: all the resources of heaven are available to us (Matthew 6:10). Jesus rose from the grave, ascended on high, and sat at the right hand of the Father. Together, He and the Father enjoy partnering with us in releasing all the resources of heaven on earth! Bondage, a fruit of wrong belief systems, can keep us from releasing those resources. Bondage is reinforced by a false mindset, an orphan mindset, a wrong identity. A false belief can lead us into a wrong feeling—a wrong feeling about God, yourself, or others. A wrong feeling can lead us into a wrong action or behavior. When this happens, our feelings are dictated by what we believe and manifest in how we believe. If we believe a lie, our feelings tell us we are unloved, misunderstood, and rejected.

All bondage is rooted in fear and that fear is believing the lie of a false identity. When we run to our heavenly Father in prayer and enter His presence with boldness, we walk in the truth of who we really are—His children with full access to His presence. When we run from our heavenly Father's presence, we will believe the lies and we can end up in bondage. Fear will cause you to run away from the Father, but knowing you are loved and chosen will cause you to run towards the Father. When you are afraid, cry out loud "Daddy God, help me, save me!"

> ...for you did not receive the spirit of bondage again to fear, but you received the Spirit of adoption by whom we cry out, "Abba, Father." Romans 8:15

When we were born again, we were adopted into the family of God. We are called to live from our true identity as sons and daughters belonging to our heavenly father. We are no longer slaves to a false identity. We believe what His word says about us, and not by how we feel or by what others say about us.

Believing a false identity reminds me of a story I heard many years ago.

One beautiful spring day, an eagle egg rolled from its nest and safely landed in a nearby chicken coop. As the sun shone brightly in the sky on that beautiful spring day and the flowers began to emerge from the earth, a passing hen noticed the lone egg laying there unattended. The hen, like all hens, chose to sit on the egg until it hatched. Soon the day approached when the egg began to crack and out came the baby eaglet. As the eaglet began to mature in the chicken coop, he started to notice that he did not feel like the other birds around him, nor did he look like them. He didn't act like the other birds around him, and he was not satisfied being confined to a coop. Something inside of him did not feel right; he felt like he was created for more.

One bright and beautiful summer morning as he was making his way out of the coop, he glanced heavenward, gazing up into the cloudless and beautiful blue sky. He saw something remarkable. High in the sky, he saw the most beautiful bird he had ever seen. As he gazed heavenward, he was mesmerized by the height the bird was flying as well as the beauty of this strange looking creature. As you may have already guessed, he was gazing upon a full-grown eagle soaring effortlessly and majestically in the sky above. As he looked heavenward, longingly he said to himself, "I wish I could be like that bird, soaring high above the earth, graceful, free, and uncaged." The problem with the eaglet was a mindset; he had an identity problem. He did not know who he truly was. He was raised in an environment that defined who he thought he was. He was captive to a lie, a wrong belief system. He needed to be told what he was created to be and what he was created to do.

We need to remind ourselves, as well as the enemy, whose we are and to whom we belong!

As fathers, we can help our children understand the difference between conviction by the Holy Spirit and accusations from satan. Most accusations comes after we have sinned, failed, or we feel like we have disappointed God. Remember, relationships are heaven's highest priority. If the enemy can get your children to believe God is angry with them, or rejecting them, there is a tendency for them to return to what is familiar, old habits and addictions.

Jentezen Franklin says, "The enemy will always attack from the last place he was successful." When this happens, we must read and speak the truth of God's Word over ourselves, regardless of how we feel or what we think. Shame wants us to focus on how we feel instead of declaring the truth of who we really are.

Shame is the tool the demonic realm uses to get us to believe in a false identity. Honor and glory are the opposite of shame. Honor is what the Holy Spirit wants to bestow upon us in order for us to live in our true identity. Conviction is meant to lead us into repentance. Conviction is agreeing with God about the condition of our sin. Conviction says, "What I did was bad." Shame tries to get us to agree with the lie that we are bad. Shame wants us to identify with our sin and believe a lie that leads us back into bondage, slavery, imprisonment, and captivity. There is a difference between a prisoner and a captive.

FALSE IDENTITY IS LIVING AS A PRISONER IN CAPTIVITY

A captive is a hostage held in slavery by someone else; a prisoner is in prison due to his or her own making. The goal of the enemy is to take us captive with lies and imprison us by our own failures, sin, and shame.

Jesus came to release captives and free prisoners (Isaiah 61:1)!

> If we confess our sins, He is faithful and just to forgive us our sins and to cleanse us from all unrighteousness. 1 John 1:9

Many times when we repent, we ask God for forgiveness and He forgives us, but sometimes we still feel the weight of shame. When I ask God to forgive me, I also ask Him to cleanse my mind with the blood of the Lamb. It is the blood of Jesus that silences the accusations of the enemy (Revelation 12:11)! Once we pray for our minds to be cleansed, we must choose to believe God's Word, not the accusing and shame-filled voices we still hear in our head. If we do not deal with shame in our lives, it can hinder our ability to walk in our true authority and calling. *Shame is locked in our heart due to the lies in our mind.*

So, it is vital that our children know their true identities. Their need to feel good or worthy about themselves is not dependent on their performance. It is a lie from the enemy to believe that acceptance is based on performance, either with God or with man. The truth of God's Word is the key to unlock the lies that afflict the minds of our families; and God's presence will heal any shame hidden deep in their hearts.

Speak destiny into your children; let them know of their great value in your eyes and in the eyes of their heavenly Father!

CULTIVATING SIGNIFICANCE

Significance is knowing that our lives have meaning, that what we do is important and that our lives matter to someone.

WHEN WE GET a correct view of Father God, we find our identity in Him. Our significance to Him as sons and daughters is fortified by the value He placed on us when sending His son to die for us. He placed His love upon us before we even loved Him or acknowledged Him, He loved us first. We were valuable to Him before we were created.

> Even as [in His love] He chose us [actually picked us out for Himself as His own] in Christ before the foundation of the world, that we should be holy (consecrated and set apart for Him) and blameless in His sight, even above reproach, before Him in love. Ephesians 1:4, AMPC

THE CROSS DEFINES OUR SIGNIFICANCE

We have freedom because of the cross. Jesus was looking forward to our salvation; we were the joy set before Him (Hebrews 12:2). Joy is something that must be always in front of us.

The freedom of the cross allows us to practice without the fear of making mistakes because the price has already been paid for all our mistakes! Punishment will always look backward; discipline looks forward. It's never about what I did, but what I'm called to do. Punishment is for the benefit of the one punishing but discipline is for the benefit of the one being disciplined. Jesus bore all the punishment we deserved on the cross, and freely gave us what He deserved. Discipline is always for our benefit. Our heavenly Father disciplines us because He loves us. We are His sons and daughters.

The fear of punishment keeps people in bondage. Slaves are punished; sons and daughters are disciplined (Hebrews 12:11).

> There is no fear in love. But perfect love drives out fear, because fear has to do with punishment. The one who fears is not made perfect in love. 1 John 4:18, NIV

The greater the love the greater the mercy; the greater the mercy the greater the kindness; the greater the kindness the greater the love!

> Or are you [so blind as to] trifle with and presume upon and despise and underestimate the wealth of His kindness and forbearance and long-suffering patience? Are you unmindful or actually ignorant [of the fact] that God's kindness is intended to lead you to repent to change your mind and inner man to accept God's will)? Romans 2:4, AMPC

The religious spirit is not kind or loving. Grace gives to us something we don't deserve, and mercy doesn't give us what we do deserve—both are gifts and not rewards. The religious spirit puts demands on a believer to work to earn a gift we've been given, and it doesn't forgive or forget when we mess up.

Gifts are given and wages are earned. God gives gifts and does not pay us the wages our sins have earned when we come to Him. Religious bondage requires us to earn our way into God's presence, or pay Him back for what He freely gave when we were saved by Him. When we require people to earn, or keep, their salvation through works, we are shackling them with religious bondage.

Religious bondage is an anti-Christ spirit. Antichrist means, "to replace with." The word "Christ" means "anointed one." So, an antichrist spirit will replace the anointing with bondage, rules, or legalism, using fear of punishment as a motivator instead of the gift of love as an activator.

> There is no fear in love (dread does not exist). But perfect (complete, full-grown) love drives out fear, because fear involves (the expectation of divine) punishment, so the one who is afraid (of Gods Judgement) is not perfected in love (has not grown into sufficient understanding of God's love). 1 John 4:18, AMP

Self-condemnation, control, and shame partner with the religious spirit in order to keep people in bondage through fear.

Self-condemnation points to the condition of your sin, but conviction leads you back to connection with the Father. Our focus shouldn't be on the sin that is in someone's life; it should be on what's missing in their life, and what motivates them towards the sin. What's missing many times is an experiential revelation of the love and lordship of Jesus. The minute someone puts the focus on "being right" instead of maintaining right relationship with Jesus, the relational connectivity is threatened. Our goal should always be pointing people to Jesus instead of pointing out their sin. As people begin to come into right relationship with God, we should help them identify sin as an obstacle that keeps them from loving effectively and from living in freedom.

A changed mind without a changed heart doesn't change a thing.

Helping people identify it's conviction they are feeling and deny the shame the enemy is trying to put on them, will be a powerful revelation in pointing them towards the Father instead of away from Him. The true nature of all sin is selfishness—and selfishness hurts people. Helping people identify where they have been independent from God due to their own rule instead of self control helps them realize they need to restore relational connectivity through repentance. Father does not want us hurting, nor does he want us to hurt one another. Repentance is coming into agreement with God about our choice to live independently from Him, and asking Him for forgiveness. It's coming into absolute dependence on God and interdependence with other believers. Walking in forgiveness is crucial if we're going to walk in our destiny. Tough conversations are needed sometimes to restore relationships, but our approach needs to be tender when confronting. Conflict does not ruin relationships; unforgiveness does.

TOGETHER WE CAN DO MORE

Living in fear causes us to make decisions that are made from an independent spirit instead of an interdependent spirit.

Trusting God and others around you is living your life interdependently. We need God—but we also need each other. Not only does God have an assignment for each of us individually, but he also has assignments for us corporately. Sometimes we place a greater value on individual destinies while overlooking the power and effect of corporate destiny. I don't believe you can fulfill your individual destiny effectively unless you are living in corporate destiny with others, working towards fulfilling a vision that's bigger than anyone could ever do alone. Corporate destiny requires right alignment which is living in right relationship and surrender if we are to fulfill heaven's assignments. There are too many independent ministries and independent churches trying to fulfill a heavenly assignment that requires the whole body to fulfill together.

It will take more than one church to win a city. When we live in fear instead of from faith we become unbelieving believers. An unbelieving believer is someone that believes in God but they don't believe God. The fear of man can become a snare and our biggest faith killer and keep us from our destiny, both corporately and individually.

BATTLING THE FEAR OF MAN

I've gone through seasons in ministry when people would leave the church I was pastoring for various reasons and fear would grip my heart. On one occasion our team had to bring some loving correction to one of our young leaders and we did not handle the correction in a healthy manner. This was because I had abducted my role as a spiritual father and released more authority to someone than I should have. If we abdicate our role of authority instead of walking in it, we relinquish power instead of delegating it.

Choosing to prioritize right relationships means we press through hard stuff, because relationships are key in everything we do. When needing to be right becomes your priority, anger, pain, unforgiveness, and the destruction of relationships will become your fruit. There is usually a pattern that the enemy uses to move us out of love and destroy relationships. His favorite tactic is the deterioration of trust. It starts with suspicion, then moves to accusation, dissension, and division eventually causing the destruction of the relationship. I see this spreading wildly through the churches in our nation. The best way to stop the descent to destruction is to deal with suspicion head on. Communicate clearly and honestly where you feel suspicion stirring up.

Many times when people leave a church, their dissatisfaction begins with suspicion in an area of unhealed pain; then if it is not addressed quickly, or is addressed incorrectly, the enemy will stir up accusation and assumptions. Most relational conflicts begin with small or unresolved issues that build over time, usually because of a lack of honest and transparent communication. (That's the fear of man.) The enemy then comes in like a lion to devour and destroy. The enemy's goal is to destroy as many people as he can, not only to impact and ruin relationships, but compromise the witness of the church in the local community as well.

When I walked through this season not too long ago, I began to question my identity as a leader. I started to believe I was failing. I wondered if maybe it was time for me to leave the church. I even began to believe that I was too old to be leading a church. Sometimes as leaders, when we see people leave the church, fear or anger begins to grip our heart.

Lie after lie began to flood my mind, and my heart was hurting as I watched people I loved walk away. My identity, significance, and influence were being tested. I believe the call that God has given me is the heart of a father for the fatherless, the orphans, and the broken. I watched in pain as sons and daughters began to leave the church, the family. I had spent hours with so many of them, helping to restore marriages, healing their hearts, helping with their bills, declaring their destinies, and pouring out my love as well as my time. My heart was broken, and deep pain inside me was being exposed again!

When the enemy attacks our identity we begin to question our significance and doubt our influence. Our core leadership team as well as many of our pastors, key leaders, and faithful members stood strong and firm in their loyalty to the vision of the church, their love for my family and me, and our leadership during this season of pruning. Their relentless love, prayer, encouragement, prophetic words, feedback, and support helped carry my family and me through this difficult season.

The betrayal during this particular season had been the greatest testing of my faith I'd walked through in ministry yet, and I've walked through many fires over many years. The Lord ministered to my heart one day when a powerful intercessor in our church looked me in the eyes and said, "Fathers don't quit, hirelings do." I went home and wept. How could I leave the people I loved, the people that God called me to, the ones who remained standing after the battle was over and the smoke had cleared?

We are a tribe, a family. I will never understand how pastors and leaders without this kind of love and support weather the storms of ministry. When we as leaders don't surround ourselves with healthy, trustworthy, real, and loving relationships we can easily become toxic leaders when we are in pain. I was in pain, and becoming a toxic leader was one of my greatest concerns.

WHEN DEPRESSION DEFINES YOUR IDENTITY

"When a leader lacks confidence, the followers lack commitment."
John Maxwell

I have taken many steps towards restoring my identity and reclaiming my significance over the years. One step has been to get away alone with the Lord in the secret place. Our confidence can only be affirmed by Him. When we are in pain we need our dad. When times are difficult, I usually get up early in the morning before anyone in my household and spend time in His presence worshiping, praying, and weeping over the pain of loss or the fear I'm battling. The second step is to begin taking inventory of how and where I could have done better as a leader. Leaders fail when they stop growing, learning, leading, and asking the right questions.

A few years ago, during a very difficult season in ministry I began slipping into some deep depression. I didn't notice my descent at first, but my wife did. I began to isolate at home, retreating into our bedroom. I found myself not wanting to preach on Sundays and I found it difficult being around people—even people that loved me. I felt deep sadness inside and I didn't trust people. Normally I could pray and worship my way out of discouragement or depression, but not this time. I felt myself slipping further into the darkness of the soul. There is a caution and a danger that I want to address here: if we spend too much time in introspection, especially when we are in isolation, we can be in danger of slipping into depression. That's exactly what was happening with me.

Isolation can give way to vain imaginations.

At one point my wife and I looked up "depression" and we read the thirteen signs of clinical depression together.

1. Trouble concentrating, remembering details, and making decisions.
2. Fatigue
3. Feelings of guilt, worthlessness and helplessness.
4. Pessimism and hopelessness
5. Insomnia, or sleeping too much
6. Irritability
7. Restlessness
8. Loss of interest in things once pleasurable, including sex.
9. Overeating or loss of appetite
10. Aches, pains, headaches, or cramps that won't go away

11. Digestive problems that won't get better, even with treatment.
12. Persistent sad, anxious, or "empty" feelings.
13. Suicidal thoughts or attempts. (WebMD)

I scored twelve out of thirteen! I was shocked and became even more depressed. How could this be happening again? I thought that when I took my sabbatical a few years earlier everything would be better.

My wife lovingly said, "I think you need help. You need to see a counselor." What I heard through my filter was, "You're really screwed up."

She wasn't being mean or insensitive; we were both really concerned, and she was simply giving her input. I shared with the core team of men I work with what was happening and what I was going to do. They gave me loving feedback and agreed that I needed to get some healing. I had become tense and frustrated, and was battling anxiety and extreme exhaustion. Weariness and fear caused me to believe the wrong things or hear things the wrong way, and then I would react emotionally. I was on my way to becoming a toxic leader.

These men were such a powerful encouragement to me and exercised great patience with me. They were more patient with me than I was with them. My emotions were out of control because I was believing lies, and my heart was responding to those lies. They all agreed that I needed to see a counselor, and I heeded their feedback as well as my wife's. I was crumbling on the inside, a duck above water paddling madly, except this time it felt like I was paddling in a typhoon!

I began to see a Spirit-filled Christian counselor who was a former pastor and a wonderful man. He told me right away that he didn't tell his clients what to do, he partnered with them, the Holy Spirit, and their spouse. His goal was to help them understand what was going on inside their brain; how it impacted their emotions and relationships. He said his job was to help me identify my emotional responses and recognize the false beliefs at the root of those responses.

False beliefs are lies that need to be replaced with truth, and God's Word is the truth. When we believe a lie, we partner with satan, and partnering with the enemy instead of God is sin. The sin is choosing to believe lies instead of God's Word. My counselor helped me identify the sin, repent, renounce the lies, and begin to replace them with the truth. We discussed and identified how I would respond to the truth regardless of how I was feeling.

I had been allowing my feelings to lead me instead of the Holy Spirit. I had to start believing the truth that people I loved were telling me, even if I couldn't believe it for myself. I also had to verbally begin declaring the truth of God's Word out loud so my ears would hear it. Faith comes by hearing—by hearing the truth spoken out loud (Romans 10:17).

WE ARE TRIUNE BEINGS

We are made up of body, soul, and spirit all working together (1 Thessalonians 5:23).

As I sat in his dimly lit office with the shades drawn for privacy, my counselor told me that once we discovered what was happening inside of my head, he would be able to help me discover the tools in order to begin the healing process in my heart. The goal was to learn how to apply the tools I would learn so I could deal with my emotional responses correctly.

(What I love about Dr. Steve is his passion to see people heal. He gets so excited about his work when he talks. He kind of reminds me of a mad scientist you find in a lab in some remote castle, giddy with excitement as he talks.) Right away I took a series of tests that defined my personality and my make up. The tests also gave us some insight as to what was going on inside of me: 93% anxious and 96% clinical depression. I was off the charts!

He then looked at me and said something shocking, something nobody but my wife knew about. "At some point in your life you were sexually abused, and it wasn't your fault!"

I stared at him, stunned. How did he know about that upstairs room, in a house three houses down from ours, where something ugly happened to me?

He repeated, "It wasn't your fault!" I began to weep right there on his couch. In a dimly lit room decades ago something horrible happened to me. Now in a dimly lit room so many years later, Holy Spirit was healing my heart by partnering with a man who was exposing my pain and lifting the shame.

The little boy inside of me had been carrying the weight of shame, and deep inside I felt like what had happened to me was somehow my fault. Because I couldn't control the situation at six years old, I grew up trying to take control of things around me as I became an adult. Because of fear, and emotional and physical abuse from my stepfather, I was too afraid to let him or my mom know about what was happening.

When I was a child growing up, my stepfather treated me harshly in a mistaken belief that it was his job to make me tough. As a result, I believed a lie that I had to be strong and ignore was happening to me. If I felt pain and shame, I wasn't being tough. Dr. Steve represented a father figure, so for him to recognize and call out my pain was healing to my heart. It had been men who hurt me, and God used a man to help bring healing.

When we feel powerless and unprotected as children, we grow up seeking control. And when things feel out of control, we react in fear and take more control, or we medicate the pain, or we shut down and learn to not feel at all. We begin to close down emotionally and protect our heart. Our heart and mind begin to disconnect with anything that causes pain. What we believe determines what we choose to feel, and what we choose to feel, or not feel, affects how we behave.

Something unlocked in my heart that day as I sat in Dr. Steve's office. I felt a new sense of freedom, but the healing was just beginning. Exposure of pain in a loving and safe environment helps people heal. I soon learned that the sabbatical I took years previously healed my heart towards my unhealthy view of, and co-dependency with, ministry. This time my healing was about childhood trauma, pain and regret, and my unhealthy view of myself. I'm so glad God chooses to heal us in layers, like an onion, peeling back one issue at a time. He is so loving and patient with us. He's such a good Father.

CULTIVATING FAMILY AS A TESTIMONY

Never let past regrets create present day roadblocks that keep you from your future promises.

FATHERS AND MOTHERS come alongside their children to develop and help them mature.

Just as our heavenly Father wants us to believe we are sons and daughters and not slaves to our sins, mistakes, or past, so should we model this acceptance and guiding mercy to our sons and daughters.

God is our Abba—our Papa. He knows when we feel the worst about ourselves is when we most need a Papa. He is Almighty God, but I personally believe His favorite title is Papa (Romans 8:15). He knows the guilt of sin makes us feel separated from Him because we've disappointed or failed Him. He wants us close to Him when we feel the most vulnerable and worthless. When my own kids are feeling low, discouraged, or like they're failing I want to do everything in my power to encourage and love on them out of what they're in. When they are feeling the most vulnerable about themselves is when I want to be closest to them. I don't want to rescue them, but I want to walk with them, value them, encourage them, empathize with them, and love them out of whatever they're in. This is what dads do. We become the arms, ears, and voice of the heavenly Father to our kids when they feel far from Him.

Your family home should be a place where you can be transparent, be the real you without the risk of rejection. The members of a family grow in love and experience comfort and healing when there is a culture of transparency, vulnerability, and love. These must be a high priority.

This kind of transparency can only operate fully in the church culture when it's operating in families. When sons and daughters are truly loved by fathers and mothers, it expands into our churches and becomes evident to the world, because love will be experienced and not just preached. I believe a wave of revival is coming and it will sweep many broken, hurting, and love-hungry people into our churches. It will be like a tsunami of God's spirit sweeping out into the streets and pulling many people into the family of God, so our churches need healthy families to invite the broken into true family.

> Above all, have fervent and unfailing love for one another, because love covers a multitude of sins [it overlooks unkindness and unselfishly seeks the best for others]. 1 Peter 4:8, AMP

I believe what's coming is a revelation of the Father's love and God is preparing His church by stirring things up and shaking things out! Hebrews 12:27 speaks of a shaking; I believe God is going to the foundations of families and churches.

For our children to feel safe and vulnerable they need to know that they will be covered—not just forgiven. Covering someone means looking past their sin, past their issues, and focusing on who they are and not on who they're not.

Two of Noah's sons covered their father's nakedness when their brother exposed it. They chose not to put their attention on what their father had done (Genesis 9:23). Noah was not a drunkard even though he was drunk. "Covering" means to protect or conceal. We cover what the enemy exposes through shame and condemnation by protecting our children's hearts. We protect their reputation by not repeating or sharing their story without their permission. We must not let familiarity become an excuse for dishonor, but instead treat our families with respect. We become a shelter or sanctuary for them when they are in danger of the enemy's lies.

We can do this when we view our loved ones through the lens of the Father's love. Jesus modeled this by covering the women caught in adultery in John 8:1-11. We literally make our homes a sanctuary or safe place, where others can be vulnerable when all the religious spirit wants to do is cast stones of judgement.

One definition for condemned is "officially declared to be unfit for use." I'm sure this is how this woman caught in the very act of adultery felt that day as she stood guilty before her accusers. Today people struggling with guilt and condemnation deep inside feel the very same thing: accusation, shame, judgement; declared "unfit to be used." People just find temporary pleasures and addictions in order to hide their shame. As fathers, we must model and teach our sons and daughters to walk in both grace and mercy, so they will know they are covered and be able to help other people heal and find mercy.

What shame cloaks people in, we uncover with grace and then cover with mercy.

> But God, being [so very] rich in mercy, because of His great and wonderful love with which He loved us. Ephesians 2:4, AMP

One way to look at grace is giving someone something they don't deserve, and mercy is not giving someone something they deserve. Many Christians can forgive someone because they know they're supposed to, but extending mercy means loving someone enough by giving them something even if they don't deserve it. That's what our heavenly Father has done with us! It is easy, sometimes, to overlook the importance of this with the people closest to us, but we should be filled with so much love that we're sowing love out of our overflow.

When we live in the well of His presence we can live our lives like a hose, saturating others with his love. We should be sowing into others the same measure of love, grace, and mercy that's been sown into us by our Father in heaven. We've been given all the Father's love without limit (James 2:13). Love can have defined and healthy boundaries but it can also have unlimited resources.

FAMILY LIVES IN AUTHENTICITY

Only in a family environment can right identity be reinforced, fortified, and developed, especially when we are going through pruning, trials, or difficult times. We were created to live in family. When you find your family you will find your destiny.

FAMILY SHOULD LOOK AND LIVE LIKE JESUS

I'll never forget the day I witnessed love that looked like Jesus. I was attending a workshop at a conference in California with about a hundred other pastors and leaders. The topic was helping people with sexual brokenness find healing. The man speaking was sharing his personal story about coming out of the homosexual lifestyle and his journey from sexual brokenness to healing. I could tell he was nervous about publicly sharing his personal and painful experiences. It takes guts to stand up in front of 100 or more pastors and expose your past with the hope that those hearing can find healing or learn how to help others heal. After about fifteen minutes of sharing his story, an older gentleman in his seventies entered the room from the back. The room was packed but he found a seat on the very front row. This older man looked as if he had just parked his John Deere tractor in the church parking lot. He was wearing overalls and a ball cap. The room fell silent as he took his seat.

As he sat, the speaker said, "I'd like to take this opportunity to introduce you all to my spiritual father and mentor."

I was stunned. I would not have ever seen them as men I would have put together, let alone in that deep of a relationship. After he introduced the man, I watched this speaker begin to relax, as he appeared to feel completely safe and comfortable sharing his heart.

What changed? It was the atmosphere of the room that day when the mentor in overalls walked into the room. The man speaking knew that if no one else accepted him, or if what he had to say was rejected, the man that walked into the room had his heart and his back. He knew he was loved and valued because the one that represented Jesus to him had just walked into the room.

This is the power and safety our sons and daughters can live in when they know love from their earthly fathers and their heavenly Father.

> Love has been perfected among us in this: that we may have boldness in the day of judgement; because as He is, so are we in this world. 1 John 4:17

Spiritual maturity is measured in how much we love and not just in how much we know.

"Perfected" in this verse means mature or complete. Maturity is loving like Jesus loves. When we are loving like Jesus we have the assurance in knowing that we are living like Jesus. We can love like Jesus because He lives in us. When we choose to yield and heal, He can love through us. God will never ask us to do anything His Spirit will not enable us to do. When we surrender to God He works through us, and when we partner with God His Kingdom advances.

There is no codependence or independence in the Kingdom; only interdependence. The Kingdom is always other-focused. Our earthly families matter to the Father.

We reproduce what we are and not what we teach.

God is always challenging us to love more like He loves. He's maturing us. Mature people give love and serve from love because they want to see others develop, grow, and fulfill their destinies. Immaturity is living in survival mode as a perpetual victim. Immature people live from the place of need, like toddlers. Toddlers need care and constant attention. They need someone to always meet their needs. As parents, we recognize that most toddlers are self-focused. Words like "mine, me, and I" are communicated frequently. The job of a healthy parent is to raise their children up to become healthy adults that are not self-centered or self-absorbed.

This carries over into church leadership, as the focus of healthy apostolic leadership is to reparent the orphan heart (Ephesians 4). Sadly, many in the church today live from immaturity and operate out of judgement and not love. Jesus rescues people from the destruction of sin's grip and He heals the pain it causes!

Out of the example of healthy family development, God is looking for spiritual fathers and mothers who are developing spiritual sons and daughters, not just building ministries, buildings, or churches. Our desire in raising up sons and daughters is never about what they can do for us; it's about what we can help them become, how we can express our love, support, and encouragement.

When we create this kind of culture, it allows our kids to dream big without feeling controlled.

According to Malachi 4:6, it's the fathers that turn their hearts towards the children first. As fathers and mothers, we must turn our hearts toward our children, as well as toward the orphans in our culture (recall the story of Tyler in chapter three), risking the possibility of being rejected, misunderstood, and abandoned. We may experience pain. It may take a lot of love and patience as well as persistent pursuit. It may take time, but we can't give up.

When we are rooted in love we are unstoppable. When we are grounded in love we are unmovable (see Ephesians 3:17).

And behold, a voice from heaven said, this is My beloved Son, in whom I am well pleased and delighted. Matthew 3:17, AMP

The Father was pleased with Jesus before He began His ministry. "Beloved Son" was the identity the Father declared and reinforced so all could hear. His pleasure and delight were that Jesus was His Son. Jesus was significant. He was important to the Father, and not just important—He was the delight and pleasure of His Father. We, too, are sons and daughters of our heavenly Father; we too are significant and important to Him. We are His pleasure and His delight (Song of Solomon 7:10, Psalm 149:4). He rejoices over us with singing (Zephaniah 3:17). Like a parent singing over a child, He sings over us because He is so in love with us and He wants all of heaven to hear it. We need to speak this over our sons and daughters and declare who they really are!

God's love is deeper than shame's deepest pit, longer than disappointment's darkest hall, and stronger than depression's tightest grip. Love never fails because it never lets go.

CULTIVATING HEALTHY RELATIONSHIPS

Religion says, "I messed up. My Dad is going to kill me." The Gospel says, "I messed up. I need to call my Dad." Rob Radosti

As fathers, our assignment in keeping relationships a high priority is to keep our hearts connected when our kids mess up, otherwise they will begin to disconnect their hearts due to fear and even self-loathing. This will keep lies deeply rooted and undetected.

Thoughts that are unchecked and unspoken in a family begin to plague everyone's mind. Fiery darts from the enemy begin to come against us (Ephesians 6:16). Thoughts of unworthiness, failure, regret, lust, and doubt. All these thoughts are at work in our minds. (There may even be some truth mixed in.) The enemy is the master of perverting the truth. Perversion may have a little bit of truth in it but perversion is always the wrong version.

Satan perverted the word of God when he tempted Jesus but Jesus untwisted it and spoke the pure word back to the enemy. The goal of the enemy regarding Jesus was to get Him to fail; the enemy wanted to destroy the destiny of Jesus and try to ruin His relationship with His Father by causing Jesus to disobey His Father (Matthew 4:1-11). The enemy tried to get Jesus to question the Father's love for Him.

This is still the goal of the enemy, trying to disrupt family relationships and ultimately enticing us to question God's love for us.

COCK-A-DOODLE -DO-OVER

We all know the story of Peter and his denial (Luke 22:54-62). Peter the rock; Peter the one who would speak before he would think at times; Peter who said he would never deny Jesus denies Him to a servant girl. Peter caved in fear because he believed a lie.

Peter failed Jesus after he promised he wouldn't. So, after the Resurrection, Peter went back to what he knew how to do, what he believed he had control of, which was fishing. He had failed and disappointed everyone. However, I love what the angel says to the women at the tomb after Jesus is resurrected. "But go tell His disciples—and Peter..." (Mark 16:7). Peter was still loved even if he didn't feel like it. Peter was isolating, and isolation gives way to vain imaginations (2 Corinthians 10:5). When our kids mess up they begin to disconnect their heart relationally in order to protect themselves from more pain, disappointment, and failure.

BREAKFAST, BREAKTHROUGH AND BELONGING

Jesus said to the disciples, "Come eat breakfast" (John 20:12). I love this! Let's just go to Denny's. I love how loving and relatable Jesus is. Let's gather around food and talk heart to heart. Let's not make this a hard or difficult conversation by focusing on how you messed up, let's have a loving conversation by creating a safe environment around food. Jesus took pressure off the disciples by cooking them breakfast first. As fathers we can take pressure off our children when they mess up. They may still need to take responsibility and clean up their mess, but they need to know that they are loved even amid the mess they made. Jesus sits with Peter after breakfast and asks, "Do you love me more than these?" (John 20:15).

What Jesus was saying to Peter was don't disconnect your heart from me; I haven't disconnected mine from you. We know this because Jesus used the word *agape* for love when asking Peter if he loved him. *Agape* love can be defined as undefeatable, unconquerable love that seeks the goodwill of the other person. It is self-giving love that gives freely without asking anything in return. *Agape* love is a love by choice and not by chance. It's a love of the will and not just the emotions. It's unconditional love.

That is the kind of love God calls us fathers to give to our sons and daughters.

81

CULTIVATING INFLUENCE, BUILDING CHAMPIONS

A loving family is an influential family.

INFLUENCE: THE CAPACITY to have an effect on the character, development or behavior of someone or something, or the effect itself (Webster's dictionary).

Jesus began His ministry at a wedding, and when He returns, everything will culminate with a wedding. Our homes should be vibrant and loving expressions of connection and unity, not look like orphanages. Orphan mindsets can be present in the home when our kids are ignored and do not know who they are, what their purpose is, or where they belong. How do we ensure that we create and steward this kind of atmosphere in our families? It all begins with us having a right identity as sons.

"I'M RIGHT AND YOU'RE WRONG" IS WRONG AND NOT RIGHT

When we make a choice to be lovingly honest with one another and put our decision to love above our feelings, we break the lie of the enemy, healing happens, and trust is built. Fathers who model this kind of transparency in their families create a culture that sons and daughter will follow. Culture is what you practice, not just what you believe. **We have to be willing to lay down our right to be right and choose to respond in loving discipline instead.**

COMPASSIONATE, LOVING CONFRONTATION, NOT COMPROMISE

Never compromise the Word of God as the standard in loving because the Word of God IS the standard for loving.

We must love our families from a position of grace and mercy, sanctified by the blood of Jesus, and grounded on the truth of God's Word. We must be cautious of an unsanctified form of grace and mercy, compromising the truth because we are afraid of making our children uncomfortable. Unsanctified grace and mercy occur when we hesitate to take a biblical stand in order to avoid loving confrontation.

There is never a need to compromise the truth or promote fear to get our children to behave or believe correctly. The power and presence of the Holy Spirit, the truth and transparency found in God's Word, can fill our homes as we love Jesus and express that love in our family interactions. **Even when correction is necessary, love and mercy creates openness for change.**

Right relationships should be our highest priority. Love is being present. Love is taking the time to really listen. When you are truly present in the moment, you will hear things you missed in the past, and you will experience a deeper level of love because you will have a new level of understanding.

INFLUENTIAL FAMILIES RAISE UP CHAMPIONS

Create your family home to be a living structure with a hole in the roof—a place without limitations! Establish a culture of people who dream big, take risks, trust God, and love and serve well. Raise up champions, not spectators. One definition of a champion is: "One that does battle for another's rights or honor." King David was a champion. He defeated Goliath to fight for the honor of Israel and defend the character of God. One of the definitions of Goliath's name means to expose. The enemy wants to expose people's shame, failures, and shortcomings. The enemy wants to accuse and slander people (Revelation 12:10-11). Champions are people who have the faith for others when they don't have faith for themselves. Champions are willing to take risks because they love well. Champions are kingdom influencers. When we raise future champions, they become influencers and champion others in return. When your desire is to influence people, do not look outward, seeking to build a ministry or program to accomplish a task. Focus on your family, to whom you minister and love.

CHAMPIONS ARE RISK TAKERS

On one occasion as Jesus was teaching, there were so many people crowding the house that there was no way to get in through the door, and there was no room left in the house. Some men, whom I would call champions, brought a paralyzed man on a mat to be healed, but could not find a way into the house. They needed to get their friend to Jesus. What they did was amazing, creative, and costly. They made a hole in the roof of the house and they lowered the man on a mat down to Jesus! They took a risk and the man was healed, physically and spiritually (Luke 5:17-39). When Jesus saw the faith of the helpers, he forgave the sins of the man on the mat. That man did not even ask for his sins to be forgiven; his only desire was to be healed. Forgiveness was the first thing Jesus did before he healed the man. *Changing the condition of the heart is far more important to the Father than just healing the body.* When Jesus saw their faith, He responded (Hebrews 11:6).

When I read this story, I have often wondered who paid to have the roof repaired? When we take risks, there is always a cost. For every problem, there is a solution; and champions look for the solutions, they do not focus on the problem. The problems do not keep them from believing Jesus can do impossible things when they take risks. Champions are kingdom influencers! Risk takers don't see problems, they see challenges. Do not let the problems become a distraction.

Distraction is the death of your dream in slow motion- Dale Bronner

A few years ago, I was preaching on this passage of Scripture and I declared that I wanted our church to be a church with a hole in the roof, where people could bring their friends into the church to meet Jesus. One of the other pastors came up to me after my message and said, "You know our goal should not be about getting people into the church but getting the church out to the people." He continued to say, "When we practice this, the hole will expand." This statement changed my focus forever and it put legs to the vision of our church. Expanding the kingdom does not mean growing your church; it is about raising up big people who take down giants outside the church! I want to raise up giant killers! Jack, the giant killer! Big hearted risk takers take down big giants.

CHAMPIONS ARE DEPENDENT ON GOD

Goliath was a giant in the land physically, but David was a bigger giant than Goliath spiritually! David was a champion. How could David be so secure in his identity? Not long before this battle with Goliath, he was overlooked, and not even invited to the lineup with his brothers when Samuel came to anoint one of Jesse's sons to be the next king of Israel. Even King Saul questioned David's ability to fight Goliath, due to his age. When he showed up to the battle, his own brothers mocked him for being there.

> And Saul said to David, "You are not able to go against this Philistine to fight with him; for you are a youth, and he a man of war from his youth." But David said to Saul, "Your servant used to keep his father's sheep, and when a lion or a bear came and took a lamb out of the flock, I went out after it and struck it, and delivered the lamb from its mouth; and when it arose against me, I caught it by its beard, and struck and killed it. Your servant has killed both lion and bear; and this uncircumcised Philistine will be like one of them, seeing he has defied the armies of the living God." Moreover David said, "The Lord, who delivered me from the paw of the lion and from the paw of the bear, He will deliver me from the hand of this Philistine." And Saul said to David, "Go, and the Lord be with you!" 1 Samuel 17:33-37, NKJV

David's identity was established and fortified in his intimate times with God. Real champions are God chasers, they are pursuing after God's heart. David was a man after God's heart. He was a passionate worshipper first and foremost. I believe that is why we are seeing so many young people drawn to worship right now and why we are seeing so many worshipers being raised up. God is getting ready to release many champions in order to take down the Goliaths in the land, the "Davids" are currently in the obscure fields, killing the lions and the bears, faithful in their intimacy with God, and loyal to the leaders they serve. David knew how big God was, and his confidence was in God's character, not in his own ability. David did not just believe in God, he believed God.

David was not concerned with the size of the problem or situation because he knew God was bigger. His confidence was not in his own ability, but in God's ability through his active obedience to God. Dependence on God means that if God doesn't show up, it's over. We need to be so dependent on God that the risks we take cannot be accomplished unless he intervenes. Dependence on God can only come from our time alone with God, pursuing his presence above pursuing our own ministry. David spent many hours worshiping God out in the fields with the sheep. David learned how to recognize the voice of God before he needed the intervention of God.

When we are raising up champions, we are looking for those who are willing to make the pursuit of God's presence a bigger priority in their lives than pursuing their own ministry. Our ministry to God must be more important than our ministry for God. In order to accomplish this, fathers and mothers must set the pace. As a father, my priority must be to spend more time alone with God than I do in working for God. My influence for Him comes from my time with Him (Acts 4:13). My time with God equips me for the assignment from God.

CHAMPIONS ARE INTERDEPENDENT AND NOT INDEPENDENT

An independent mindset is an orphan mindset. When families are disconnected, children grow up feeling like orphans, not sons and daughters. Too many churches operate the same way. Many prodigals outside the church walls do not want to be sent back to the orphanage, so they choose to live independently instead of going back to religion with control and performance at its core. Too many potential champions have been hurt and used by the church simply to drive church programs, not advance the Kingdom. Like David, they were told they need to wear the king's armor instead of being released and coached to flow in their creative freedom and be allowed to use their slingshot.

CHAMPIONS HAVE APOSTOLIC FATHERS AND MOTHERS, NOT JUST INSTRUCTORS

If you release authority based only on how people perform, then you will create a structure that has performance at its core.

> For though you might have ten thousand instructors in Christ, yet you do not have many fathers; for in Christ Jesus I have begotten you through the gospel. 1 Corinthians 5:15

All fathers should be teachers, but not all teachers are fathers. True apostolic fathering is more about coaching and guiding than it is instructing and telling. As already noted, true apostolic churches have a high value for building families, not just building an organization or a program, but building people. A family is a body of owners, not members. Costco has members, but a family has relationships. Families have inheritance, sons and daughters who are owners and partners. It is not a membership, there are no yearly dues. Sons and daughters are loved, developed, empowered, and released, and not just used to build a "business."

Fathers empower sons and daughters by taking pressure off. Weight and responsibility are not the same thing. We give away responsibility. Weight creates pressure that causes fear and produces performance. Responsibility has clear boundaries with expectations but there should be no fear or pressure that the relationship will be damaged or threatened if there is failure in not fulfilling the responsibility.

There are three main elements when empowering people. They are called the three rings of empowerment, and as we see our children growing in maturity, we begin to recognize and nurture these elements as we give them greater freedom. The elements are: Authority, accountability, and responsibility. Authority without accountability leaves young people unfocused. Accountability without responsibility leaves them unable. Responsibility without authority leaves our kids unmanaged.

If we give our children too much leeway in decision-making, empowering them without all three rings in place, it creates a weight in their lives. The weight can either become dangerous, damaging, destructive, or all three.

FATHERS AND MOTHERS ARE THE GUIDES AND NOT THE HEROES.

I was at a conference not too long ago where Donald Miller, a well-known author, was speaking. He was talking about what went into writing a good story and the need to be good storytellers, because everyone wants to hear a good story. He shared about the different characters in a good story and the roles they play. Two main characters he talked about were the guide, and the hero or heroine.

As fathers, we are viewed as heroes in our young children's eyes, but as they mature we are called to guide them into becoming the "heroes" of their life story. The hero is the person in the story that needs to overcome some kind of obstacle, personal challenge, or crisis. We are called to coach and raise up heroes. With the help of wise guides, they find their purpose and meaning and overcome the obstacle, destroy the villain, rescue the persecuted, and save the day. The apostle Paul was the guide while Timothy and Titus were the heroes he raised up. Paul saw himself as a spiritual father to a young Timothy (1 Timothy 1:2).

Influential families do not foster insecurity, because each member understands their personal as well as family identity, and they realize don't have to perform to earn it; they can just "be," make mistakes, and learn without the fear of being criticized or unloved (1 Corinthians 11:1). With the guide's help, the hero transforms into a champion for the Ultimate Hero—Jesus Christ.

TRANSFORMATIONAL FATHERING

And He will turn the hearts of the fathers to the children, and the hearts of the children to their fathers, lest I come and strike the earth with a curse. Malachi 4:6

THIS IS A prophetic verse about apostolic fathering and it applies to what God is desiring in His church family. It is about fathering a fatherless culture. We are currently experiencing the curse of fatherlessness in our world right now. The lack of right identity and one living in shame instead of significance are the results of this unhealthy influence. In contrast, the culture of heaven is the culture of family. If our mandate is to bring heaven to earth, then family is a part of that mandate (Matthew 6:10).

To raise up champions with a healthy family foundation, every church and ministry must recognize, confirm, and empower apostolic leadership who will speak into our church as well as into the lives of the leadership for accountability. Apostolic leaders may either be a part of the church or outside the church, but they come alongside the leadership of that house in an ongoing relationship. For example, I operate in our local body as an apostolic leader, but

I also have an apostolic father outside our church who speaks into my life regularly, as well as into our church and our leadership team. I give apostolic leadership to other churches, ministries, ministry and business leaders as well. I come alongside in relationship to encourage and empower others (1 Corinthians 4:15).

If we father and mother accurately, people will love effectively.

Apostles carry the weight of government, prophets carry the oil of intimacy and insight, teachers carry the depth of revelation, pastors carry the burden for the sheep, and evangelists carry the fire of miracles and reconciliation. – Ryan LeStrange

I believe apostolic fathers along with a five-fold ministry team must identify, train, empower, and release multiple pastors (shepherds) and five-fold leaders as defined in Ephesians 4:9-16. In recognizing, empowering, and releasing the office gifts within the body, the apostolic leaders have the time to father effectively. In the American church, the pastor is typically identified as the lead voice in the church. In a church operating in the five-fold ministry, the apostle is recognized as the father and lead voice in the house. The word apostle literally means "sent one." Apostolic churches raise up, release, and send others into the "fields of harvest." Apostolic churches are like families that empower and raise up sons and daughters who transform culture. Like fathers who affirm and establish right identity within their children, *apostolic leaders recognize, raise up, and release people to impact the world around them.* Being an apostle is not about a title. We never use titles or ask people in our ministry to call us by a title. We put the emphasis on the character and the operation of the office or gift. Those who operate in true five-fold offices will, by the Holy Spirit, recognize others who carry office gifts as well. Relationship is always the focus and never the position, anointing, or title.

We relentlessly focus on maintaining right relationship as the highest priority of heaven and constantly strive to build a culture of family in our church. In doing so, you can actually feel and see family in the atmosphere when we gather corporately.

FATHERING FLOWS FROM THE TOP DOWN

My greatest role is to be an apostolic father to the leadership team, and they in turn release that to the leaders they oversee, and it overflows into the body. Because we have made right relationship a focal point, we protect and maintain this culture distinctive, even as the church continues to grow or people choose to leave. If I shift into a management or caretaker mode instead of leading, the atmosphere shifts. I experience fear and the people around me sense it. If I feel the need to take control in order to see results, I forfeit my rest and become restless. We must walk in rest as leaders, not just physically, but spiritually and emotionally as well. If I maintain my peace, I will walk in rest. I must vigilantly guard my peace, daily and sometimes hourly!

FATHERS LIVE IN AND MAINTAIN PEACE BY LIVING IN REST.

And let the peace of God rule in your hearts, to which also you were called in one body; and be thankful. Colossians 3:15

In this verse, the word rule literally means "to umpire." Let peace be the umpire of your heart and let peace call the shots! When I shift into a worry and negativity mode, I begin to lose my peace. When I shift into thanksgiving and praise, I get my peace back. Never allow the storm on the outside to become greater than the peace on the inside. Jesus could sleep during a storm because, deep inside, His confidence in His Father was greater than the conflict going on outside of Him (Matthew 8:23-27).

Jesus was secure in His identity and He was confident in the Father to fulfill His destiny. We need to be careful we don't find our confidence in our destiny and allow it to define our identity. Confidence always manifests as peace. Self-confidence will manifest as control, rooted in pride instead of humility.

FATHERS AFFIRM VALUE

Transformation changes the value of the vessel due to what it carries.

It was like any other wedding—dancing, gifts, friends, vows, family, and love. It was like any other wedding, except that this wedding was about to experience a miracle that only a few guests would even know took place. The wedding was in Cana and Jesus was one of the guests (John 2:1-11). Ordinary water pots become extraordinary that day. They once contained ordinary water, but at the word of Jesus, they contained premium wine! The value of the vessel changed, due to what it contained. If ordinary people are made in the image of God, they contain value and worth that needs to be identified, and drawn out, transformed by the power of Jesus's word and blood. Jesus told the servants to fill the pots up to the brim with water, and then get pitchers to serve the guests. What came out was not just good wine, it was the best wine. *Obedience to a revelation brings about transformation.* When leaders are obedient in helping people experience personal revelation, transformation can take place. Personal revelation begins with a heart connection to truth.

FATHERS PLACE A HIGH VALUE ON TRANSPARENCY

I encounter many people who have been hurt, felt used, or received wounds from leaders in the church. Some wounding is due to the fact that many people are in rebellion, and refuse to repent or deal with their own junk. Unfortunately, much of the pain people deal with has often been caused by the unhealed pain within a leader's own life. As the saying goes, "hurt people hurt people." Fear and insecurity foster isolation. Isolation is dangerous, especially for leaders. Accountability is crucial if you are going to be an agent of healing and transformation for others. Leaders need to be in true and real accountability with other leaders. They need the feedback from others to deal with the pain and junk in their own lives before being able to confront lovingly and assist people in pain. As we heal, we can help walk others through healing without judgement. Fathers need other men for accountability and friendship. I am a part of a local pastor's group where I share my church struggles and my prayer requests. I have many friends and I even have spiritual mentors. The key to getting healthy is in getting transparent with other trusted leaders. I cannot stress this enough!

There was a time when I was not in transparent relationships with other men I could trust. My fear of being vulnerable at that time was due to the fact that I had been hurt by people in the church and my heart was guarded. The only person who saw me for who I really was, was my wife, and she felt the pressure I was carrying. Like me and so many other pastors, the only person with whom they are open is their spouse. Because I would share my own pain and frustrations with my wife, she would hold her own pain inside as she did not want to add more pressure to my plate. There are far too many couples for whom this is the case. Wives feel as if there is no one with whom they can safely share about what their husband is going through, for fear of betraying him. Many ministry wives sit alone in silence, watching their husbands suffer in pain, anger, frustration, or loneliness; and they do not know how to help or what to do about it. Many fathers and leaders carry the weight of the world on their shoulders. They feel trapped, but they love the Lord, and know they cannot forsake their gifts and callings. But when hearts are entirely submitted to the Holy Spirit, they are no longer guarded by fear due to unhealed pain.

FATHERS ARE IN RIGHT ALIGNMENT

For my family and me, the needed transformation took place as God revealed the blueprints of apostolic leadership to me and to our leadership team. We implemented this form of government into our church leadership structure. Our structure transformed from being a pastor-led church to an apostolic-led church, and the weight and pressure of ministry began to lift off my shoulders. As the weight lifted and I got healthy, so did my wife and my family. I went from managing a church to truly leading the church. The transformation was not easy and there were some challenges, but the fruit outweighed the struggles. My greatest role in leading the church became to define the "why" we existed as church, instead of being the one to answer the how and what we do as a church. (A great book to read regarding the why of leadership is *Start With Why* by Simon Sinek).

I moved from the role of insight and oversight into prophetic foresight. Foresight is looking ahead to what God is doing regionally and globally, and then communicating to our team and to the church body why we are important in fulfilling His Kingdom plan. I also reinforce our family culture and our vision every time I preach or teach. The second role to which I am called is to be a father. I am called to love, encourage, raise up, and come alongside sons and daughters, both inside and outside our local church, and support what God is doing in them and through them. In this role, I teach, help cast vision, support, and develop leaders. As an exhorter, I recognize the gold in people. Before the fivefold leadership was in place, I would empower people before they were ready to bear the weight of certain ministry responsibilities. This only set people up for failure. But now, with the fivefold team working together, we complement and balance one another in our callings. We work together in leading the church by developing, empowering, and releasing the body.

FATHERS ARE IN ONGOING ACCOUNTABILITY AND ENCOURAGE OTHERS TO BE AS WELL.

As an apostolic team, we continue to disciple all our leaders, and all our leaders disciple others as well, not just oversee a ministry or department. We call it LLT— Loft Leadership Team. (The Loft is the name of our church.) We also require all of our leaders to be in a small group called Life Groups. These groups spend time building friendships together, not just ministering together. When we truly love each other, we can lead well because we lead from love. If a leader is too busy to take the time to build and maintain ongoing friendships, they are headed for burnout, blowout, or worse. Many leaders spend most of their time ministering, and not enough time in building healthy relationships with other leaders, mentors, and friends, which is why so many leaders burn out.

Unhealthy leaders tend to make ministry assignments more important than relational alignment, mutual submission, and honor. God is always focused on relationships first (Matthew 5:23-24). Heaven's assignments become more prevalent and powerful as we come into alignment with one another.

In our church, the office of evangelist works alongside the office of the pastor to make sure that the new believers, or sometimes, unbelievers coming into our church, find family and get connected. The evangelist and pastor work together in order to make sure people are discipled, taken care of, equipped, empowered, and deployed. *The true office of evangelist is concerned about the care and the development of the lost once they get saved, not just in seeing the lost get saved.* The office of the evangelist is also instrumental in working alongside the pastor in getting the church body outside of the four walls and into the lives of others, loving and reaching the people we encounter every day, whether at work, school, home, or play. Signs, wonders, and miracles are a high priority to an evangelist, but so is nurture, care, and the ongoing development of new believers. New believers grow best in those small groups that function like families. The fivefold office helps to identify, develop, and release multiple pastors to minister in our church and in the marketplace. We train them to help take care of the needs of the body in their small groups. Everything from hospital visits, prayer needs, to the tangible needs of the body are all taken care of by the small group family and their pastors. We also reinforce, teach, and cultivate our church culture, as well as call out the gold (exhort or prophecy) over one another in our small groups.

Instead of one pastor, churches should have multiple pastors caring for the needs of the body. This is the Jethro principle found in Exodus chapter 18. Our pastors are shepherds. Though they may not necessarily preach or teach from the pulpit, they disciple and give care to small groups of people, like smaller churches within our body.

It takes time to build, implement, and maintain this type of leadership structure. We have been working on building an apostolic eldership team for years now, and will continue to refine and define our structure. It takes time because it is not just a team you interview and hire. It is entirely built on prayer, fasting, and lots of time together, building trust. We invest ourselves wholly into establishing and strengthening relationship with one another; it is our highest priority.

There have been bumps, bruises, and some blood along the way, but the victories and testimonies outweigh way the challenges. It's never easy to make relationships the highest priority of heaven in your church or ministry. When you determine to keep relational connectivity at all costs, it will require time, work, patience, forgiveness, flexibility, confrontation, love, and healing. It will cost a lot!

Convenience and sacrifice cannot coexist. It is either about my comfort or the comfort of another (John 15:13).

The book of Acts, chapter two, describes something beautiful taking place when the church functions in apostolic leadership.

> And they continued steadfastly in the apostles' doctrine and fellowship, in the breaking of bread, and in prayers. Then fear came upon every soul, and many signs and wonders were done through the apostles. Now all who believed were together and had all things in common and sold their possessions and goods and divided them among all, as anyone had need. So they continued daily with one accord in the temple, and breaking bread from house to house, they ate their food with gladness and simplicity of heart, praising God and having favor with all people. And the Lord added to the church daily those who were being saved. Acts 2:42-47

Many times I have read this passage, saying to myself, "I want to be a part of a community like this!" Our church is not there yet, but that is my blueprint and our goal. We desire deeper community, healthy leadership, growth, right biblical structure, favor with the community, power evangelism followed by signs and wonders, meeting tangible needs, and souls added to the church daily. Did you notice it was the Lord that added people to the church, not expensive programs, gimmicks or marketing? It is not only possible to have a church just like this, it is where the Lord is leading His church in these days. When leaders make it their determination to focus on church health, instead of church growth, those churches will become healthy and grow into maturity.

FATHERS DESIRE UNITY AND NOT JUST AGREEMENT

And God has appointed these in the church: first apostles, second prophets, third teachers, after that miracles, then gifts of healings, helps, administrations, varieties of tongues.
1 Corinthians 12:28

This verse, as well as Ephesians 4:11-16, gives an idea of the order of the offices and their alignment. When biblical, apostolic structure is in its proper place, heaven's assignments will be released and the fruit of new souls will be experienced. When the government of heaven is in place there will be unity! Unity is different from oneness. In John 17:21-26, Jesus prays that His people would be one as He and the Father are one. Oneness precedes unity. Like in a marriage, the more a couple becomes one, the more they will experience unity in the marriage. This then has a powerful effect for unity within the family. When we individually become one with the will of the Father concerning His will, we can flow in unity with one another.

Within our family relationships, it is never about my will, it is about His will. To be one and walk in unity requires purity. Oneness is the result of something being one hundred percent pure, with nothing else being added to it. Unity is having one heart, walking in alignment, but carrying out different assignments.

Never get things out of order; and if you do, make the adjustment to get things back in order. The order of your family as a demonstration of the Kingdom of God is always love first. Pursue love above the gifts or anything else. Desire spiritual gifts and ask for them, but do not make the pursuit of gifts, offices, titles, or ministry your goal. Be a father first, and always pursue love. We are pursued first by the Lover of heaven so we will surrender to His love. Why then would we want to pursue what He gives us, instead of who He is?

CONCLUSION

Hold on to hope because God always keeps His promises

WHEN WE CHOOSE to put Him first, He prunes everything in our lives that keep us from loving effectively and accurately. His desire is our healing and our wholeness so we can fully love as we are fully loved.

It was the message every parent dreads: "Michalea has been in an accident!" I was at a leadership meeting the day I received the call from my wife regarding our oldest daughter. She was a passenger riding in the front seat of a pickup truck when suddenly a six-and-a-half-pound rock came flying through the windshield and hit her in the forehead, shattering her skull. My daughter slumped over in the front seat bleeding, as the driver of the vehicle pulled into a church parking lot so he could call 911.

Michaela has always been in love with Jesus as long as I can remember. She has a passion for worship and she pursues the heart of God. She is a goal setter and she dreams big; even as a child she set goals for herself. She goes after what she wants and has a heart wired for travel. Years ago, when Michaela was around nine years old, she came bouncing out of her room one day telling her mom and I that God had told her she would go to Africa. We both smiled, patted her on the head and said, "That's wonderful sweetheart!" We really didn't pay much attention to that simple statement until she started decorating her room with an African motif and then sponsored a child from Africa with her own money. She even started raising money and giving it away to African missionaries.

It was then that I knew she was serious and she had heard from God. I'm a slow learner.

After receiving the phone call regarding her accident, I drove to the hospital that dreadful day, not knowing what I would find when I would arrive. I remember crying out to God in prayer alone in my car, scared and desperate. All I could picture in my head was my sweet little girl as I begged God to spare her life. She was only fifteen years old. We had dedicated all of our children to the Lord when they were born and we know that they are His and not ours, but in that moment, when you're facing the possible loss of a child, it's extremely difficult and painful to let them go and keep reminding yourself that they're not really yours. I cried out to the Lord that day in my pain and fear of losing my daughter. In my agony I remember telling the Lord that I would still follow Him, serve Him, and love Him regardless of the outcome.

It was then, in that split moment of crying and in complete desperation I heard the Lord say, "*She has not gone to Africa yet and I always keep my promises.*" God promised a nine-year-old girl that she would go to Africa and He doesn't lie. I knew at that moment she would live. I had hope in the fact that God honors His word, even when things look like they're at their worst. There is always a big difference between believing in God and *believing God*. That day I believed God and held Him to His promise after I heard Him speak to me.

Miraculously, my daughter was released from the hospital after surviving a blow to the head that caused a subdural hematoma— bleeding near the brain. She was in ICU for twenty-four hours, and the hospital for only four days. After surgery and multiple screws and stitches she was released to go home. She came through with no side effects except occasional headaches. She eventually went back to high school and graduated with a four-point GPA.

At twenty-three she went on her first, but not her last, missions trip to Uganda! *When God gives you a promise not even hell itself can stop it or take it from you as you cling to it!* God has promised us that He is coming for a glorious church that He is building and He will fulfill His promise (Ephesians 5:27).

All the promises God has given us He will fulfill. Our part is to walk in obedience, submission, and right relationship with Him and with others. We get the amazing privilege of partnering with Him in ministry to see His Kingdom come and His glory released! He builds His church and we partner with Him in that work. When we know our true identity, understand our significance, and partner with Holy Spirit to be an influence, our labor in the Kingdom flows from a place of rest. When we rest He works; when we toil and work in the flesh He rests and waits. Could it be that much of the breakthrough we are wanting to see in our cities, regions, and the world is because God is waiting on us?

THE KINGDOM IS A KINGDOM OF FAMILY

History started in the garden with a family and ends at a wedding feast in heaven. I started this book with my daughter standing in the kitchen telling me she felt like I was more of a pastor than a dad. This is the same daughter that survived the accident. Losing my daughter in an accident would have been unimaginable, but losing my relationship with my daughter would have been unbearable. Too many leaders and their families are being taken out by the enemy. Too many leaders and their wives battle loneliness, deep pain, and weariness, and are running on empty. God is such a good Father and He doesn't want slaves, He wants children and friends.

My desire in writing is to see fathers and leaders get healthy, get help, and get encouragement. My desire is to see leaders get healed and healthy, so they can establish right relationships around them within their churches and ministries.

A church family is only as healthy as its leadership. Changed people help people change and changed people change cities. Jesus changed cities and regions during His time on earth, not by holding big crusades, but by changing people one at time and leaving them in their cities to impact their businesses, schools, and communities.

His biggest impact was on twelve disciples He walked in relationship with on a daily basis—deep and vulnerable relationships.

I have tried to be as vulnerable and as transparent as I could in this book because I love fathers and leaders. My heart aches when I see families destroyed because of the unhealed pain. I see weariness and discouragement in many pastors and leaders, especially now. I've been there and I still walk through times of pain, hurt, discouragement, and occasionally, fear. But I don't walk through them alone anymore or believe lies. I don't hide from these times; I don't run from them because now I am surrounded. I'm surrounded by real, healthy, transparent relationships. I'm held by love in the arms of my heavenly Father as well as in the hearts of friends, co-laborers, and a family that genuinely loves me and challenges me to *be* my best, not just *do* my best. I've been loved greatly and I owe the world an encounter with the same love I've been loved with.

We all do.

"Great faith is the product of great fights. Great testimonies are the outcome of great tests. Great triumphs can only come out of great trials." Smith Wigglesworth

REVIEW AND RESOURCES

1. Knowing your true identity is key to establishing and maintaining right relationships.

2. Significance is never found in what we do; it's found in what Jesus has already done.

3. Everyone is a leader. The first person you lead is yourself. If you're a father you lead your family by example above all else.

4. If you're hurting get help. Isolation reinforces lies. Hurting people only hurt others.

5. True accountability is deeper than friendship; it's interdependence.

6. Building trust is the key to all healthy and loving relationships. It may take time but it's worth the investment.

7. Replace lies with truth. You can either empower lies or walk in truth—regardless of how you feel.

8. Spiritual maturity is always other-focused and measurable by how we love God and others.

9. Build yourself, your family, and others as a priority above your business, career, or ministry.

10. Walk in authenticity, transparency, and vulnerability. Remain teachable.

11. Spend ongoing and deliberate time in God's presence. Presence is far more important than performance.

Resources for accountability and spiritual growth:
    The Identity Project.
    https://kingdomliving.global/

Books:
    The Heart of a Warrior—Michael Thompson
        (Heart and Life Publishers, 2016)
    Boundaries—Henry Cloud, John Townsend
        (Zondervan, 2017)
    Sifted—Wayne Cordeiro, with Francis Chan & Larry Osborne
        (Zondervan, 2012)

ABOUT THE AUTHOR

JACK SHUMATE HAS spent over thirty-five years in ministry. Jack has pastored in small and large churches and ministered to youth, young adults, and adults. Currently he is serving as one of the senior leaders at The Loft in Oregon City, Oregon. Jack has a desire to see churches grow healthy and not just grow numerically. He believes it's not about the size of your church, ministry, or following—but it's about the size of your influence. It is vital to raise up big people, not just big ministries.

At one time Jack was a pastor at one of the fastest growing churches in the nation with over five hundred home churches in the city of Portland, Oregon. Today Jack and his wife Shelly live on two acres in the beautiful Mount Hood foothills in Oregon. Jack and Shelly have six grown children. Jack has a strong call and desire to come alongside pastors and leaders to mentor and encourage and help them get healthy in every area of their lives.

You can email Jack at jack@influentialleadership.info or visit the website: www.influentialleadership.site.

CPSIA information can be obtained
at www.ICGtesting.com
Printed in the USA
LVHW020958090622
720769LV00015B/1620